The Essential
30 Core Elements ship

n, in writing or by
number on
red

1

The Essential Manager: 30 Core Elements of Leadership

Enda Larkin

Chartered Accountants Ireland

Published by
Chartered Accountants Ireland
Chartered Accountants House
47–49 Pearse Street
Dublin 2
www.charteredaccountants.ie

ISBN: 978-1-908199-72-0

Typeset by Datapage
Printed by Turner's Printing Company, Longford, Ireland

Contents

Introduction

"The dogmas of the quiet past are inadequate to the stormy present. The occasion is piled high with difficulty, and we must rise with the occasion. As our case is new, so we must think anew, and act anew."

Abraham Lincoln

I like this quote, an extract from an address given to Congress by Abraham Lincoln in 1862. Although the context was very different, I think his words could just as easily be applied to the world of work today – and specifically to the role of managing. It is not an exaggeration to say that we must look again at all aspects of how we manage with a view to improving. Of course this is nothing new. Management has always been an evolving art; it can never stand still but must adapt in response to changing circumstances. Therefore, a key ingredient in the recipe for management success is your ability to move with the times. And in recent years the times most certainly have moved. No matter at what level you currently manage, be it in the private or public sector, you know only too well that the ground has shifted beneath your feet. Your performance is likely coming under greater scrutiny than ever before from superiors and you increasingly need to get the most from your people – who, by the way, are also demanding more from you. On top of all that, you must keep your customers or stakeholders satisfied in the most competitive marketplace ever seen. It's a big ask, but that also makes it a great time to be a manager, if you like a challenge that is.

Recent developments have also seen a more healthy air of realism return to the topic of management than existed even a few short years ago. You know the kind of thing I am talking about. For a while there it had reached the point where style seemed to matter more than substance when it came to the manager's role. It could even be argued that the term 'management' went out of fashion as everything centred upon 'leadership'. You will no doubt have heard talk of transformational leaders, organisational champions and even extraordinary heroes who were supposedly leading us all towards a professional Promised Land. Thankfully, a lot of that hyperbole has now disappeared, and whether it's called 'management' or 'leadership' is of little practical concern these days, because results are all that matter. That's a welcome development in the evolution of management thinking.

On that issue of terminology, if you really think about it, who cares anyway whether you are called a 'manager' or a 'leader'? What is far more relevant is what you do in practice every day. Irrespective of the management role you hold, to excel you must be able to balance three interdependent components of work: people, process and performance. In other words, you need to engage your people and focus on process in order to achieve the required results. And doing so actually requires you to both lead (engage) and manage (achieve). You simply cannot be fully effective today without balancing both these functions. Too much 'leading' might help you motivate your people, but doesn't necessarily mean you will achieve the expected results, just as too much 'managing' might get things done, but at the risk of losing some or all of your employees along the way. So, when you get back to basics about what the manager's role entails, the answer – at least in principle – is surprisingly straightforward: you must lead and manage and you must do so consistently well. As you read ahead, the terms 'leader' and 'manager' are often used interchangeably, but are always meant in the sense of someone who can competently balance both roles.

Considering the limited time and resources available to most managers for self-development, I felt there was an urgent need to provide something of real value to help all managers master the lead-manage challenge under the demanding conditions faced now and into the future. And that's the rationale behind *The Essential Manager*: it is intended as a topical and practical resource for all managers which addresses pressing issues in an easy-to-read way. In writing it, my intention was not to add to the list of 'how to' management texts, or to get bogged down in jargon, but rather to focus on helping you to better understand your evolving and expanding role.

When I started this book, I sat down and listed all the questions that managers repeatedly raise with me during the many development workshops and mentoring sessions that I hold. Then, to get a sense of whether I was on the right track, I showed that list of topics to a wide variety of experienced managers, to see if they reflected their current concerns. With a bit of tweaking here and there, I finally arrived at a collection of 30 essentials. These are not necessarily all the issues that matter to you, nor are they especially new, but they certainly are the core building blocks of management success.

As a result you will find a wealth of down-to-earth guidance in the pages ahead which encourages you to reflect upon, and perhaps consider changing, how you currently respond to some common trials and tribulations (and joys) of managerial life. The 30 topics are presented across three dimensions which directly impact upon your ability to shine:

Part 1 – *About You* begins with a focus on you, because you can never hope to bring the best out of others until you first get the most from yourself.

Part 2 – *About Employees* concentrates on important aspects of leading and managing your employees, who are, after all, the people who can help you to achieve your personal and business goals.

Part 3 – *About Business* is concerned with some key activities associated with managing any business or function. For instance, it addresses subjects very much to the fore at present, like strategic planning and managing change.

Many of the topics covered across the three dimensions are interlinked and, as in the natural world where the single elements within the periodic table combine to form more complex substances, the subjects explored here are not only important individually, but also in association with others. For example, one early theme addressed is self-awareness, which is naturally vital in its own right, but when considered in conjunction with other essential components, such as communication, the combined impact makes you more effective at engaging your people. It is this interdependence of the 30 essentials which makes *The Essential Manager* a unique resource in terms of comprehensively informing your self-development efforts.

And why should you take any heed of what's presented here? I have had extensive management experience so I know exactly what it takes to balance the competing demands that any role can bring. Added to that, I have been a management development consultant and strategic advisor working across a range of industries, and continents, including the Middle East, Europe and the US for over 20 years. I am acutely aware of the current (and likely future) challenges you face, and have learned a lot along the way from great managers about how to tackle them. Finally, in preparing each topic I conducted extensive research to identify the views and opinions of eminent thought leaders to give a solid theoretical foundation to everything covered here. As a consequence, the book intertwines theory and practice in a meaningful way.

By design, the 30 essentials presented are intended to get you to think, but I make no attempt to suggest that there is only one way to manage, one right answer, one size fits all. My only recommendation is that you reflect upon the content covered and, based on those reflections, that you consider how you can get better at what you currently do, and this applies regardless of your level of experience in the management game.

I hope you will enjoy reading this book as much as I did writing it.

EL
Geneva, Switzerland
February 2013

About
you

Think about your personal skills and attributes

Mi rror, Mirror on the Wall

"Mirror, mirror on the wall, who is the fairest of them all?"

We all remember that scene where the queen flies into a rage when she learns that someone else had surpassed her in the looks department. We remember too how it set off a chain of events as the queen sought to rid herself of the competition, with Snow White fleeing harm's way and shacking up with seven bachelors who lived together in a small house way out in the woods. But that's another story.

Beyond fairy tales, there are parallels to be drawn in real life from the *mirror mirror* incident in terms of how we view ourselves. None of us likes to think that someone else is 'fairer' than we are. Replace 'fairer' with more 'skilful', 'intelligent', 'effective' or indeed any work-related adjective and the message is still the same. We generally don't want to see ourselves as second best, or as having limitations when compared to others. As Arsene Wenger memorably responded to Sir Alex Ferguson's taunt back in 2002 that his team were the best in the league, "Everyone thinks they have the prettiest wife at home."

Management is a journey and success on that journey necessitates continuous personal development which in turn requires you to face up to who you are – to acknowledge your strengths but also to highlight your shortcomings. In an influential article in *Harvard Business Review* Peter Drucker wrote:

> Most people think they know what they are good at. They are usually wrong. More often, people know what they are not good at – and even then more people are wrong than right. And yet, a person can perform only from strength. One cannot build performance on weaknesses, let alone on something one cannot do at all.[1]

Self-awareness isn't something you hear discussed all that widely amongst managers although in truth it should be top of any list of 'must-haves' and especially so in these challenging times. When you possess high levels of self-awareness this means that you can better identify what you are good at, but also where your areas for improvement lie. As a result of that understanding of self, you are then more likely to try to minimise the impact of your weaknesses and indeed work to eradicate them over time. Unfortunately, the issue of self-awareness can seem a bit on the trivial side for some managers. In addition, a willingness to open up about areas where you feel you struggle, or even reaching out for help with them, can be misinterpreted by some as a sign of weakness, when in reality such action should always be seen as a strength.

[1] Drucker, "Managing Oneself" (2005) January, *Harvard Business Review*, pp. 100–109.

1. The Johari Window

Research, and indeed common sense, tells us that the best managers have what could be called a unique selling point; they know themselves well, understand their behaviour patterns and, more importantly, they take proactive steps to manage how they act and behave. It is this action-orientation towards personal improvement, based on their self-awareness, that sets them apart. A powerful and easy to understand tool that highlights the importance of feedback to building self-awareness in a management context is the Johari Window.[2]

This model was developed by American psychologists Joseph Luft and Harrington Ingham in 1955 whilst they were researching group dynamics at the University of California, Los Angeles. It has since become a widely respected and applied framework in a variety of scenarios, from supporting self-analysis to exploring human interactions in general, as well as being a helpful tool for understanding the impact of communication on relationships. The Johari Window can also make sense of just how different top managers really are when it comes to truly knowing what makes them tick. It is particularly beneficial in that regard because it translates what is clearly a complex topic into relatively understandable terms.

The Johari Window, shown in the figure below, consists of four panes or quadrants based on the interaction of what is known/unknown to *self* and what is known/unknown to *others*. When you think about it, there are aspects of your personality that you are open about and other elements that you tend to keep to yourself; at the same time, there are things that others see in you that you may not be aware of. The resulting matrix can help to explain human interactions and communication in general, but in this case let's explore it in the context of the importance of self-awareness for managers.

Figure 1.1   **The Johari Window**

Johari Window		Self	
		Known to Self	**Unknown to Self**
Others	**Known to Others**	**Public Area**	**Blind Spot**
	Unknown to Others	**Hidden Area**	**Unknown**

[2] Luft and Ingham, "The Johari Window, A Graphic Model of Interpersonal Awareness" (UCLA 1955).

The four panes denote:

The **Public Area,** sometimes called the arena, or open area. This relates to information/feelings/behaviour about yourself that you are fully aware of, and that others also know about you. You are comfortable with the fact that others are aware of these things.

The **Blind Spot** comprises information/feelings/behaviour about yourself that others are aware of, but about which you are unaware.

The **Hidden Area** comprises information/feelings/behaviour that you know about yourself, but which you keep from others for various reasons.

The **Unknown Area** comprises information/feelings/behaviour which both you and others are unaware of. This is the most complex area and might at one level include unknown talents or abilities, but it could also entail repressed or subconscious issues.

One of the important underlying assumptions associated with the Johari Window is that, as the public area between you and another person or persons becomes proportionately larger, the potential for positive and valuable relationships increases. Also, since the model is dynamic in nature, the panes within your window may change in size as a result of expansion or contraction of knowledge between you and others. In particular, the public area may be enlarged in one of two ways: when you open up to others, in an appropriate manner of course, about personal information that was previously unknown to them about you, this has the effect of reducing the hidden area. Alternatively, when you take the initiative to learn more about how others view you (i.e. search for feedback) this has the effect of reducing what was unknown to you, thereby decreasing your blind spot.

When you do make concerted and regular efforts to actively gather constructive feedback, and if you are also comfortable with disclosing information about yourself to others, then the combination of those facts would mean that your Johari Window might shift to look something like that shown in the figure below.

Figure 1.2   The Johari Window – The Effects of Feedback and Openness

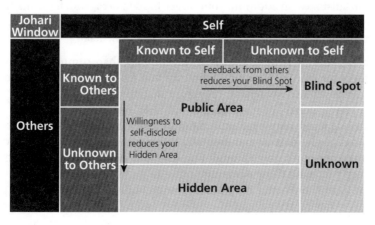

The combined effect of your openness to feedback and willingness to disclose to others reduces both your blind spot and hidden area; you therefore have a larger public area. This in turn leads to you having high self-awareness which means that you are not unconsciously behaving in ways which have a negative impact on others. Over time, you build up a very clear picture of where your strengths and areas for improvement lie and, as emphasised, you do something with that knowledge.

However, if you are less interested in, or comfortable with feedback, or if you don't have the same capacity to be open with others then your Johari Window might look something like that shown in **Figure 1.3** below.

Figure 1.3   **The Johari Window – Effects of Lack of Feedback and Openness**

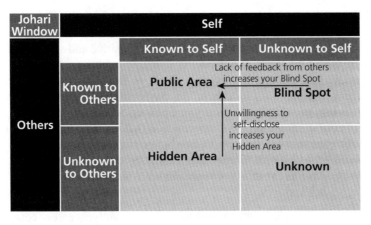

The consequences of having a small public area are twofold. First, your larger blind spot would mean that you lack self-awareness and simply do not recognise your failings, so your capacity for self-development is limited; and, as a result, you would likely continue to do the same things that cause you to under-perform across a number of dimensions. In other words, you keep blindly stumbling over the same obstacles time and time again because you do not learn from your mistakes. In addition, your larger hidden area, which results from an inability to really share and relate with others, would also mean that the relationships you forge were shallower and by nature less beneficial.

The Johari Window is undoubtedly more complex than summarised here, but this suffices for our purpose, and wherever you find yourself in terms of your current levels of self-awareness, recognise that there are a number of related forces at play which if not responded to can hold you back as a manager:

- On the one hand, employee expectations of their managers today are becoming increasingly more demanding and this trend is set to continue, recession or no recession; it's only through knowing and developing yourself that you can keep pace with those demands.
- Linked to this, the better companies have recognised the tangible and proven benefits of having truly engaged employees and this places significant pressure

on individual managers to genuinely connect with their people – and this partially means opening up to them and being willing to listen to their feedback.
- On the other hand, your superiors too are likely calling for better performance results from you all the time, so again you can only respond to that challenge if you continuously get better at what you do.

To respond to these drivers, the best managers appreciate the need for self-awareness as the foundation stone of personal development.

2. Take a Look in the Mirror

Now, it is clear that to really develop your understanding of what you do well, and not so well, you need feedback from others, but if you can be as objective as possible about your own performance then you can begin to ponder your strengths and areas for improvement. In doing so, there is no model of the perfect manager against which to benchmark yourself, but here are some key traits and skills – in no order of importance – that are seen in all effective managers. You should reflect upon how you currently perform against each of them as you read ahead. The best managers:

- *Exude energy and enthusiasm* Some people are energy vampires. They can suck the life out of you and dealing with them is draining at the best of times. Not so as far as effective managers are concerned: they do the opposite and make others feel energised and engaged, not in a trite seize-the-day sense, but in such a way that interacting with them just feels good. However, it is also important not to go too far with your attempts to energise others. In fact, as an example of what not to do here, I would suggest that you take a look if you can at a video of Steve Ballmer, CEO of Microsoft on YouTube called "Steve Ballmer going crazy". I am sure you will agree once you see it, even allowing for cultural context and his undoubted playing to the gallery, that sort of behaviour is just embarrassing. Very, very embarrassing.

  Exuding energy and enthusiasm is not about 'hooping-and-hollering', or pretending to be something you're not. It's about having the ability to raise the spirits of others, or lift people when they're down, but doing so in a way that fits with your character and indeed the culture of where you work. This trait has always been important, but with your people likely feeling under a lot of pressure right now, in their personal and work lives, you need an ability to boost them more than ever.

- *Have a knack for communication* Good communication is the lifeblood of effective management, simple as that. The best managers have a natural talent for communicating and, apart from the qualities and skills they possess which help them to interact well with others, they follow a simple but golden rule when they do so: the ABC rule, or Accuracy, Brevity and Clarity. There is nothing worse than a waffler; someone who struggles to get their point across, or a manager who simply likes the sound of his or her own voice. If you can't communicate well, you can't manage well.

- *Are always reaching higher* The best managers constantly set the bar higher in terms of their own performance; they never settle for second best and are self-motivated and goal-orientated individuals. And they expect the same of others too. That said, they are fair in the way they demand that extra effort from those around them – they don't believe that everyone else should be 'just like them' – but they demand that extra mile.

- *Visualise and get 'buy-in' for business goals* Effective managers are never head-less chickens, nor are they spineless individuals who avoid difficult issues, sit on the fence or shift positions to suit whichever way the wind is blowing. Manag-ers who excel have a clear idea of where they want the business, or that part of it for which they are responsible, to go – and those views are formed based on solid evidence with a bit of intuition thrown in for good measure. When that 'vision' is clear, they flesh it out and modify it with their senior people if neces-sary until they feel certain it is the right way to go. Then, they can win support for their vision and later can translate those broad aspirations into meaningful goals, strategies and plans which serve to engage people and guide their actions.

- *Are smart and have good judgement* High performing managers are smart characters but not always in an academic sense, although that naturally helps. However, regardless of their educational qualifications, they are individuals who benefit from having different forms of intelligence: they can analyse and solve problems, they are technically proficient when it comes to their job, they can be creative and so on. Added to that, they always seem to have a fair help-ing of that critical, if somewhat intangible, commodity called common sense.

- *Are not afraid to step outside their comfort zone* The best bosses are those who are not afraid to try different things. New is good, as far as they are concerned, if it means potentially achieving better results. At the same time, they don't for one minute imagine that they have all the answers, or that only they can identify the best way forward – far from it. Instead, they are open to taking calculated risks in the first place which means they can push boundaries, but in doing so, they also excel at harnessing the knowledge of those around them to the point where ideas and suggestions are welcomed from many sources and the flow of creativ-ity is encouraged throughout the business. They recognise that the manager's role is not necessarily to have all the right answers but to know how to find them.

- *Empower people* A lot of managers talk about 'empowerment' these days, but it's often just that, talk. The best managers do it for real because they recognise that genuinely including people in the running of the business delivers better results. They understand that when people are empowered in a meaningful sense they feel valued and respected and because of that they give more, or at least the majority do. In the eyes of effective managers, everyone is given a chance to participate and contribute; however, those who don't play their part are never tolerated for long.

- *Learn as they go* Some management books portray 'top' managers as infallible experts who rarely put a foot wrong. This is, of course, entirely inaccurate. Sure, the best managers may make fewer mistakes than others do, but that's largely due to the effective, and inclusive, decision-making processes they adopt in the first place; and when things do go wrong, these managers see such events as learning opportunities and move on. Importantly, however, they do not make the same mistake twice.

- *Follow their moral compass* In recent years there have been many examples of once-lauded executives who have spectacularly fallen from grace. While they all crashed and burned for different reasons, a big factor in their downfall was that they each lost their moral compass or they never had one in the first place.

   If you don't have a moral compass (or in other words, if you lack a set of values and rules to guide you), this can lead to a host of problems such as greed taking precedence over ethics. In other words, 'self' starts to matter most. Any number of things can go wrong when you lose sight of your values and it always leads to negative outcomes. The best managers, at any level, have a moral code and, more importantly, they follow it. They can tell right from wrong (and not necessarily in the religious sense). Still, simply knowing the difference does not a good manager make. In fact, most people can make the good–bad distinction. What sets the better managers apart is that they *choose* to do the right thing, even when that choice can come with many downsides attached; for example, deciding to recall a defective product even when the risks are low, rather than putting profit before people.

- *Possess great self-control* This is a really important trait that all stand-out managers possess. It's vital because it helps you in so many aspects of what you do. For starters, it allows you to think clearly which helps in decision-making and that in turn results in fewer mistakes. It also enables you to act rationally not emotionally when faced with difficult people or situations so you can decide which management style is best to apply in any given scenario. In general, the ability to maintain self-control helps the best managers 'think' first, then 'do', which makes them far more effective.

While this is not an exhaustive list of the traits of the best managers, these items would definitely feature on any list of management 'must-haves'. If you're 100% honest with yourself, when you reflect upon each of these areas, you can start to edge yourself forward in terms of building self-awareness.

I'll leave you with a quote from Abraham Maslow, the renowned psychologist, who once said "whereas the average individuals often have not the slightest idea of what they are, of what they want, of what their own opinions are, self-actualizing individuals have superior awareness of their own impulses, desires, opinions, and subjective reactions in general."

In other words, the best managers are not afraid to look in the mirror.

At the End of a Needle

Apparently, there is a new craze sweeping Wall Street. Well, perhaps 'craze' is the wrong word; 'crazy' might be a better way of describing it. The growing trend was reported in the *Financial Times*, and it makes for interesting reading to say the least. In the article,[3] a doctor of osteopathic medicine, Dr Bissoon, explained how an increasing number of patients were attending his clinic: "Since the recession started, more guys want to be on top of their game", he said. And what are the executives – his patients – actually doing to stay 'on top of their game'? Queuing up to get shots of testosterone from the good doctor. Yes, you did read that correctly: *testosterone*!

As reported in the article, Dr Bissoon also says that when he first started offering testosterone therapy he thought most of his clients would be avid gym users hoping to build Arnold Schwarzenegger-style physiques. But no, the majority of those attending turned out to be upper-level managers in their thirties and forties, most of whom are involved in the finance industry. Very little surprises me at this stage about the mad, mad world of high-finance, and particularly the trading end of it, but this really does beggar belief. What's more, if this is reflective of the predominant mindset amongst financial high-fliers, it's probably no wonder we have ended up in the global financial mess we're in.

Now, especially for the female readers amongst you, don't believe that there isn't a strong message here for you too. In fact, for all managers the lesson should be clear – the factors which drive personal performance at work cannot be found at the end of a needle, or indeed in any quick-fix format. There are, however, many useful models and frameworks which help to explain what is required to succeed in life generally and specifically in a work context.

One area that is getting a lot of attention recently is the growing research on Psychological Capital, or 'Psycap'. Over the past decade or more, the field of psychology has begun to place far greater emphasis on defining, in measurable terms, what it is that enables individuals to flourish and maximise their growth potential. This general research in turn has been advanced by organisational psychologists seeking to identify what helps people to excel in a work setting. Psycap is one model which provides an answer to that very question. It captures quantifiable success factors and there is now an expanding body of evidence which shows that individuals with high Psycap consistently outperform those with lower levels of it. As such, it is a concept worthy of consideration by all managers, regardless of your level, industry or indeed gender.

[3] Wallace, "Keep Taking the Testosterone", *Financial Times*, 9 February 2012.

Four components of Psychological Capital have been identified by a number of leading experts in this field.[4] They can be briefly summarised as:

- *Hope – willpower and 'waypower' to accomplish a goal* In this context, 'hope' refers to the determination and ability to set and achieve goals. So, if you have high hope, you are good at pushing yourself for greater achievement.

- *Self-efficacy – personal confidence to successfully complete a task or objective* High levels of self-efficacy, or more simply self-confidence, lead to enhanced performance because you are more assured that you can fulfil tasks, or succeed in your role than if you lack the same confidence.

- *Optimism – personal assurance of a positive outcome* This is fairly clear – the more optimistic you are, the more likely you will believe in constructive outcomes from your efforts, and be able to influence others in a positive way.

- *Resilience – The ability to bounce back in the face of adversity* A person who displays this quality is tenacious and as such keeps going in the face of seemingly impossible obstacles and odds.

Of course, we all need a variety of talents and skills to succeed, but what the research is showing is that individuals with higher levels of Psycap (the combination of the above four elements) are more confident, better able to manage stress and adversity, have a higher level of motivation, as well as being more likely to pursue growth and development. Most importantly of all, there is plenty of concrete evidence to show that those with higher Psycap consistently outperform others. One study[5] explored the relationship between psychological capital and performance and the researchers demonstrated that personal levels of Psycap changed over time, which supports the notion that it is something that can be developed, and also that it was directly linked to an individual's success. The higher the level of Psycap, the better their overall results. If you want to improve your own – and indeed your employees' – performance, you therefore cannot ignore the concept of Psycap, especially in a business environment where the need to get the most from yourself and others is so great.

Or, if that sounds too much like hard work, you could always give Dr Bissoon a call.

---

[4] Luthans, Avolio and Youssef, *Psychological Capital: Developing the Human Competitive Edge* (Oxford University Press 2007).
[5] Peterson, Luthans *et al.*, "Psychological Capital and Employee Performance: A Latent Growth Modelling Approach" (2011) 64 *Personnel Psychology*, pp. 427–450. This material is reproduced with the permission of John Wiley & Sons Inc.

Always Look on the Bright Side of Life

"43 Signs That The London Olympics Will Be A Complete Disaster."

"Why The Latest Eurozone Bail-Out Is Destined To Fail Within Weeks."

"US Heading Over The Fiscal Cliff."

"Ireland Likely To Default."

"Is The World Set To End On December 21st?"

These are just some of the headlines that caught my eye over the past 12 months. Thankfully none of them proved accurate, at least not yet, but they do serve as a reminder that some people, and not just headline writers, can allow themselves to be consumed by negativity on occasion. Times continue to be tough, no matter where you live or what you do, but focusing only on the downsides when faced with any sort of challenge isn't helpful. Yes indeed, mindset does matter during times like these. Of course, positive thinking alone won't solve the global economic crisis, or sort out our banking problems and, no, it won't put food on the table either, but it does make a difference what outlook we hold – individually and collectively – and that principle applies whether we are talking about a country, or an organisation. Unfortunately, there is still a lot of negativity floating about these days, far too much if you ask me.

While the idea that mindset matters is certainly not new, it is becoming a lot clearer now the impact it can have on performance and achievement – and as a manager, that is something you should take particular heed of. In her bestselling book *Mindset: The New Psychology of Success*, Carol Dweck, a leading Professor of Psychology at Stanford University, demonstrates how mindset makes a real difference to performance. She outlines her thoughts on the issue:

> For 20 years, my research has shown that the view you adopt for yourself profoundly affects the way you lead your life. It can determine whether you become the person you want to be and whether you accomplish the things you value.[6]

One of the most compelling aspects of Dweck's work is that it is solidly research-based, unlike much of the *go-get-'em* nonsense you read from self-help gurus,

---

[6] Dweck, *Mindset: The New Psychology of Success* (Ballantine Books 2007).

which seems to have been plucked out of thin air. On that basis alone, it is worth reflecting upon.

Dweck highlights that there are essentially two types of mindsets, 'fixed' and 'growth'. A person with a *fixed* mindset believes that the skills and competences they are born with are what determine their potential for success. You either have a talent for something or you don't; and if you don't have a particular skill or competence, then there is no point in wasting time and effort trying to master something new. It's better to make the most of what you have. For me, this is a mindset that only sees limitations and boundaries.

On the other hand, with regard to the *growth* mindset, Dweck argues that this way of thinking views anything and everything as being possible. If you lack a skill or competence, then go learn or develop it, do whatever is required, no matter how difficult. Everything is achievable. This mindset is about constantly stepping out of your comfort zone to improve and develop. And even if you do fail, that too can be a source of learning. For me, this mindset is all about possibilities.

Although her Fixed/Growth mindsets relate to how an individual views their potential for personal development and advancement, it's a great description of the divide you see in people's attitudes right now – even among some managers. You find many people who are upbeat, wide awake to the challenges that lie ahead for certain, but optimistic nonetheless; and then there are others, like some headline writers, for whom the end is always nigh. Which mindset best describes you most of the time?

Of course, it is not only your overall mindset that matters in terms of your performance but also how you view the management role itself. Two leading experts in this area, Jonathan Gosling and Henry Mintzberg, made the point very well about the diverse talents and thought processes needed by effective managers when they introduced "The Five Minds of a Manager". First of all, as I argued in my introduction to this book, they too make the case that there is no separation between the leading and managing functions and, in fact, strongly argue that it is dangerous to view them as being independent of one another because:

> Just as management without leadership encourages an uninspired style, which deadens activities, leadership without management encourages a disconnected style which promotes hubris. And we all know the destructive power of hubris in organizations.[7]

To succeed in such an expansive role as management, Gosling and Mintzberg argue that individuals must have strengths across what they term 'five mindsets':
- Managing the self (the reflective mindset)
- Managing organisations (the analytic mindset)
- Managing context (the worldly mindset)
- Managing relationships (the collaborative mindset)
- Managing change (the action mindset).

[7] Gosling and Mintzberg, "The Five Minds of a Manager" (2003) November, *Harvard Business Review*, pp. 54–63.

They also promote what is a very valid proposition that a manager must be able to combine all these five mindsets to be effective when they conclude:

> Imagine the mindsets as threads and the manager as weaver. Effective performance means weaving each mindset over and under the others to create a fine, sturdy cloth. You analyse then you act. But that does not work as expected, so you reflect. You act some more, then find yourself blocked, realizing that you cannot do it alone. You have to collaborate. But to do that you have to get into the world of others. Then more analysis follows to articulate the new insights. Now you act again – and so it goes as the cloth of your effort forms.[8]

It is the sheer depth and breadth of talents and thought processes required to make it as a manager that exposes individual weaknesses, because it is naturally hard for any one person to have strengths across all five areas, but it is precisely those strengths that are needed more than ever now.

So, to conclude, the best managers are obviously special individuals in terms of how they look at the world generally, and specifically in how they see the management role itself; nonetheless, for all of that, they are born on Earth not Krypton, or at least they leave the tights and cape at home every morning.

You become what you think.

[8] *Ibid.*

Shocking Stuff

If someone told you to act in a way that you knew would hurt another person, would you do it? No? Absolutely sure about that, are you? Think about it. If a recognised authority figure told you to push a button, which you knew would deliver a mild electric shock to another person every time they made a mistake, would you? You might do that, right? I know I probably would. But, if that same authority figure told you to push a different button which they said would severely shock – and perhaps even kill – the person, would you do it then? Absolutely not, you say? Me neither. No one would ever knowingly do something as perverse as that, would they?

In the 1960s, Professor Stanley Milgram from Yale University conducted a series of experiments[9] – you may well have heard of them – which researched the effect of authority on obedience. Essentially, the background to the experiments was as follows. Milgram and his team solicited local volunteers for what they said was an experiment on learning. When each of the selected volunteers arrived for their appointment, they were met by two people – a research scientist dressed in a white lab coat, and another 'volunteer' (who was actually one of Milgram's team). The researcher then proceeded to explain the study to the 'two' volunteers.

The real volunteer was told that he or she would be the 'Teacher' and the pretend volunteer would be the 'Learner'. The researcher explained that they were exploring the effects of punishment on memory. The task of the Learner was to learn a series of words and the Teacher's role was to test the Learner's memory of those words and administer electric shocks for each wrong answer. And they were told that, for every new wrong answer, the voltage would increase. The Teacher and Learner were then placed in adjacent rooms. On the instrument panel in front of the Teacher was a device which had different buttons, each signifying shock levels from 15 to 450 volts, along with words such as 'slight shock', 'moderate shock', all the way up to 'Danger: Severe Shock', and, finally, a worrying "XXX". During the experiment, the Learner – who could be heard through the thin wall – was also told to grunt at 75 volts; complain at 120 volts; ask to be released at 150 volts; plead with increasing vigour; and let out agonised screams at 285 volts. Eventually, in desperation, the Learner was told to yell loudly and complain of heart pain.

---

[9] Milgram, *Obedience to Authority: An Experimental View* (Reprint edition, Harper Perennial 2009).

So that, albeit very briefly, was the scenario. You get the picture. If you don't know about these experiments, then you are probably wondering what the results were? Well, under some circumstances, 65% – yes, that's two-thirds – of the Teachers were willing to progress to the maximum voltage level, regardless of the distress they could hear in the adjacent room. Prompted by the researcher, that proportion of volunteers went all the way, even to the point where they believed that they had potentially killed the person next door. Sure, many were distraught about what they were doing, but they still did it. They kept following orders. All very frightening, really.

You may wonder what all this has to do with day-to-day life for managers, but I think there are some obvious, and also more subtle, lessons to be drawn from these experiments that are worth noting. For example, a big factor in the outcomes seen in the Milgram experiments was the general environment created – the white-coated respectable authority figure, the side-by-side rooms that allowed for expressions of pain to be heard, the pressure to continue, etc. In light of this, I think it's worth reflecting upon how the work environment created can, intentionally or otherwise, influence behaviours. And often not for the better. Here are three examples of what I mean.

1. How You Use or Abuse Power

This is perhaps an obvious conclusion. At one level, the implications from the Milgram experiments are fairly clear: managers, as authority figures, can exercise their authority in a positive or negative way. But, apart from their management style and its effects on others, what about the general environment that managers create for those around them? The majority of managers I know don't intentionally set out to create workplaces where people would knowingly harm others, but sometimes this is precisely what happens, at least emotionally speaking:

- I have seen countless examples where the boss has hassled his or her managers to such an extent that they then take out their frustrations or stress on others. Dog bites cat and so on.
- I have seen sales people under such pressure to hit targets that they have knowingly sold products or services to clients who did not actually need them.
- I have seen accountants put under the cosh to make the numbers look good to the extent that applying a bit of 'creative accounting' becomes an attractive proposition.
- I have seen managers take a dislike to an individual, and I have then watched how others did the same to that person for no apparent reason other than to stay in the boss's good books.

I could go on, but you get the point. Few managers intentionally set out to harm others through the exercise of their power, but some do just that. Think about those types of concerns in relation to your business. Is power and authority generally used for the good?

2. How You Appear

This is a less obvious conclusion drawn from the experiments, so here's the link. The Milgram experiments, and others too, have shown that the appearance of authority is just as powerful as the authority itself; the 'man in the white coat' and the fact it was 'Yale University' all created an air of formality and respectability to the experiments which directly influenced the behaviour seen. But, forget about scientific studies for a moment and think of all those hidden-camera-type shows you've seen whereby somebody gets set up by what they believe is an authority figure of some kind. You therefore should be aware of how your own appearance can influence the way in which you are perceived by others and bear that in mind in terms of how you project yourself. Do you look the part?

3. How You Treat Mistakes

This is another point that relates to the impact that the overall environment can have on behaviour. Let me explain by means of highlighting another piece of important research. One group of eminent professors studied hospital unit teams[10] and found that the better-performing teams actually had a higher rate of reported errors than the lower-performing ones. That seemed impossible. Further research then revealed that the reason for this was that the higher-performing teams had developed a greater bond and stronger levels of trust and openness between them, so they were not afraid to admit their mistakes; in fact, they saw them as learning opportunities. On the other hand, the lower performing teams were hiding their mistakes from each other because they did not feel secure enough to own up to them.

If there is a lack of trust in the work environment where you manage, or if the general culture is one of punishment and retribution, then this may lead to negative behaviour patterns of some sort. Think about how mistakes are currently treated within your business and how that might be influencing behaviour.

The focus here has been to highlight that there are many ways in which the conditions you create as a manager can influence behaviour at work – and it's not just about the styles of management you adopt. Many of the things you do, or don't do, in terms of how you structure and manage various aspects of the business can negatively influence behaviours seen, or sway how people think and act; and that's the last thing you want right now when you need each and every one of your employees to operate at full capacity.

You should reflect on such matters in order to avoid any future shocks.

---

[10] Edmondson, "Learning From Mistakes Is Easier Said Than Done: Group and Organizational Influences on The Detection and Correction of Human Error", 32 (1), *Journal of Applied Behavioral Science*, pp. 5–28.

Acting the Manager

"Last night's opening preview of Broadway's most expensive production ever was an epic flop, as the $65 million show's high-tech gadgetry went completely awry amid a dull score and baffling script..."[11]

This is how the *New York Post*'s theatre critic described the show *Spider-Man: Turn Off the Dark* back in 2010. (The production got lots of publicity because it was backed by Bono and The Edge from U2). And this critic wasn't alone either, for the show was initially beset with a host of problems and was generally slated across the board by all-comers. Fast forward to December 2011 and the show raked in nearly $3 million in just one week, breaking all sorts of records. It now looks set to become one of the highest grossing productions of all time. What do critics know?

But what does this have to do with anything even remotely related to management? Well, quite a lot really. After all, if you think about it, managing others is somewhat akin to being on a stage, isn't it? For starters, you have an audience: employees, superiors, colleagues, customers and so on, and out there under the spotlight your talents, and more importantly, your failings are magnified; there is no hiding place. And, of course, there's always plenty of critics around to snipe at your performance; everyone's an expert when it comes to management. What's more, any of your failures on the management stage can be as costly – relatively speaking – as a Broadway flop, in terms of the pain caused to you, or others, and indeed the harm done to the business. And, just like any actor, you are only ever as good as your latest performance; there's always pressure to deliver.

So, drawing parallels between acting and managing works quite well actually and many of the factors that contribute to success on the stage can be applied too in the context of management. Here are a few examples, in no order of importance, of what I mean:

1. Own the Stage

You often hear it said that a good actor, or actress, must 'own the stage', or in other words, he or she must capture their audience from the outset and keep them captivated. As a manager, you too must own your stage in the sense that you need to win over those around you – your audience if you like – and this applies to subordinates, colleagues and superiors. And just like the actor who fails to grab the crowd, if you don't bring your people along with you, then you too will face a fairly excruciating experience and no doubt some lousy reviews to boot.

[11] Riedel, "First 'Spider-Man' Preview Filled with Problems", *New York Post*, 29 November 2010.

2. Have Natural Talent

Clearly, not everyone has what it takes to make it in the acting world. The same applies to management. Just as there are traits and skills that make the top actor stand out, so too are there for the best managers. And, in a management context, can those traits and skills be learned? To an extent they can be, but there must be inherent natural talent too, particularly when it comes to the traits required, for they are not so easily learned. Of course, they can be developed over time – if they are in place to some extent – but you can't, for example, 'teach' a manager to suddenly have empathy for others; yes you can increase an individual's awareness of the need for it, but developing empathy would take quite some time at best. On the other hand, the skills of management can be more readily developed, or at least enhanced, if the motivation to do so is there. As a manager, you need to have strengths across four sets of skills:

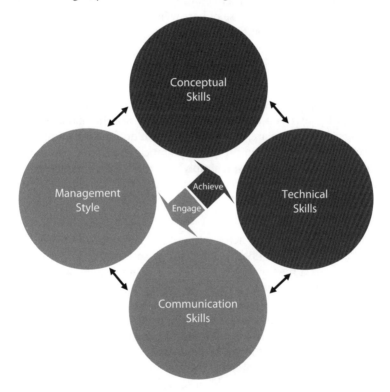

It would be laughable to suggest that every manager can master all these skills to the same degree, but you do need to have some talents in all these areas and especially so in the current climate when the challenges you face are so diverse:

- *Conceptual*: You must be able to see the big picture and ensure that the business, or your area, is consistently in tune with a changing operating environment. You need to be able to recognise and analyse complex issues, problem solve and make the right decisions.
- *Technical*: You must get to grips with the range of technical skills such as planning or financial management relevant to your level and role in the organisation.

- *Communication*: You need to communicate effectively so that you really connect with others.
- *Management Style*: You must adjust how you deal with, and respond to, the rollercoaster ride that is life in any business today.

3. Embrace the Role

Some actors take 'embracing the role' to the extreme. Daniel Day-Lewis, in an interview in the *Telegraph Magazine,* once explained what it was like when a role came to an end for him:

> The last day of shooting is surreal. Your mind, your body, your spirit are not prepared to accept that this experience is coming to an end. You've devoted so much of your time to unleashing, in an unconscious way, some sort of spiritual turmoil, and even if it's uncomfortable, no part of you wishes to leave that character behind. The sense of bereavement is such that it can take years before you can put it to rest.[12]

I'm not suggesting that you need to become as obsessed about what you do in order to succeed, but you do really need to 'get into' the management role to truly excel at it; you can't just leave the manager behind as you exit the building every day – management is more than a job. Yes, you can and should leave the stresses or hassles after you as you head home, but not the management mindset. A manager is who you are, not something you do for a set number of hours in any given day and success in the role is as much about how you think as it is about how you act and behave; you simply cannot flick on a mental switch each morning and hope to morph into manager-mode.

4. Have a Script

It goes without saying that an actor without a script wouldn't necessarily be a compelling attraction – ad-libbing can only go so far in terms of keeping the audience glued. As a manager, you too need a script, a plan, a way forward – with clear focus – if you are to successfully bring others along with you for the journey. That said, having a script doesn't mean that you won't have to improvise on occasion – improvisation is good, and necessary, once you have an overall framework or direction to keep you on track. And that direction can come from a number of sources: for the business as a whole, or your part of it, you need an overall vision and strategy as well as an annual business plan to guide you. On a personal level, you should have defined goals to focus your actions and all decisions you take should be related to those goals. Even with your team, there should be clear goals and plans agreed so that everyone knows what the collective aims are. It is through having direction that you can bring the business, and yourself, back on track when circumstances force you to deviate from what was planned.

[12] Hirschberg, "Daniel Day-Lewis: The Perfectionist", *Telegraph,* 8 December 2007.

5. Never Give Up

Very few actors succeed at the first attempt. In fact many never 'succeed' at all, but still spend a lifetime on the stage out of love for the craft. One of the most interesting aspects when you look at the career paths of many successful actors is the number of setbacks they had to overcome before the big break materialised. Management life too is full of hurdles and an essential trait needed is the ability to bounce back when things don't go as hoped.

6. Hit Your Mark

An important feature of acting is the need to constantly 'hit the mark' – where marks are set up specifically to guide an actor on stage or on set. The first step towards success for any actor is therefore hitting their mark, and to do that they actually need to know where those marks are. For managers, replace 'marks' with 'targets'. It is critically important for you to know what your targets are in the first place and of course you then need to actually deliver on them. Just as the actor failing to hit the mark will affect the show, missing your targets will be equally as damaging to overall performance.

While there are clearly some interesting parallels to be drawn between the world of acting and management, it's important not to go too far with the analogy because there are some theatrical traits that just don't translate very well into the world of management, such as too much ego or 'neediness'. Yes, all of us have a bit of ego and there's nothing wrong with that in moderation, but when a manager starts wanting to be the most popular person in the room, or seeks to hog the limelight, then it's time to exit stage left.

Th is Is Not What I Wanted!

If you owned a beautiful château in France you'd probably be pretty pleased. You might want to spend much of your hard-earned cash returning it to its former glory. You might even employ some local builders to do the work. In clear terms, you'd explain to them what you wanted (including a request to knock down an old outhouse on the site), give them the necessary drawings and plans, and then you might head off and leave them to it. After all, what could possibly go wrong?

Well, quite a lot actually if newspaper reports are to be believed. Château de Bellevue is, or should I say *was*, a beautiful property near Bordeaux. It was owned by a multimillionaire who employed a team of builders to complete agreed renovation works. Unfortunately, the owner, having communicated his wishes to the builders, went away during the planned works only to return to find that, instead of knocking down the small out-building on the site as requested, they had actually levelled the whole château, leaving only a field of rubble in its place. Local media reported that the construction company had misunderstood the owner's wishes. That's putting it mildly.

We all know that communication breaks down frequently in life, generally and within organisations, leading to minor and major consequences, and no matter how experienced you are it's worth reflecting upon this aspect of your role. While clearly there are many dimensions of organisational communication to consider, the focus here will be on two specific elements:

- Back to basics
- Style

Before addressing these two areas, however, it's important to highlight a broader issue about human interactions and particularly how some people seek to project themselves when they communicate in groups. Interesting research related to this issue was conducted by Cameron Anderson and Gavin Kilduff from the University of California, Berkeley,[13] which offers valuable insights into how some people think and behave when interacting in groups.

Using two simulated work-related experiments, and controlling for variables such as the influence of gender that might have skewed the results (they only constituted all male or all female teams), Anderson and Kilduff showed that in group situations the more dominant individuals consistently exerted higher

[13] Anderson and Kilduff, "Why Do Dominant Personalities Attain Influence in Face-To-Face Groups? The Competence-Signaling Effects of Trait Dominance" (2009) 96 *Journal of Personality and Social Psychology*, pp. 491–503.

levels of influence over the remaining participants. (No surprises there.) In the first exercise, 68 graduate students were divided into four-person teams and given a fictitious task to complete in a defined time period. After the teams performed their work, the members of each group rated one another on both their level of influence on the group and, more importantly, their level of competence. The work sessions were videotaped, and a group of independent observers performed the same evaluations, as did Anderson and Kilduff.

Following the first exercise, all three sets of judges came to the same conclusion: that those who spoke more frequently and offered more suggestions were subsequently perceived as being the most competent. (Again, nothing too surprising there perhaps.) What was most revealing in the study was that the dominant characters continued to rate highest amongst their team-mates and the independent observers even when the suggestions they made were no better – and sometimes far worse – than others.

In a second study, conducted with a new team of volunteers but following the same team format as previously, the exercise was based on the ability to solve maths problems; the idea being that some degree of competence would be required in maths to enable participants to speak up, and as such it was assumed this would influence who became the dominant players within the groups. Yet again, the researchers found that those who spoke up most frequently were subsequently described by their peers as leaders and were considered to be the maths experts in the groups. But, the researchers proved that, in fact, these dominant individuals were neither the smartest nor the ones who offered the most correct answers – what they did do was offer the *most* answers.

In a nutshell, this study highlighted that the more dominant an individual appears to be (and that doesn't have to be in an aggressive manner either), the more likely their peers are to assign attributes of leadership and competence to them. A lot of people in my experience, including managers, work from similar beliefs about dominance; they know that if they project themselves as the strongest or brightest person around then few will challenge them. And they partially do this by hogging the limelight in group communication scenarios where they seek to dominate interactions. It is worth reflecting upon whether this is something you do personally, or allow others to do to you.

1. Back to Basics

Effective managers are always great communicators. And they see the value in having regular and structured communication with their people, individually and collectively. That said, they are less hung up about the quantity of communication than its quality because they know that the more meetings employees have to attend, or the more time they spend in meetings, the more pressured they are likely to feel. Double those feelings if the meetings are badly run and unproductive. As a result, top managers make sure that what they do in terms of communication – across a variety of channels – is not only structured and ongoing, but productive too.

Effective communication is a challenge at the best of times but the workplace, with its multitude of distractions, pressures and personalities raises the hurdles exponentially. Add to this mix the one or two individuals who choose not to listen, or intentionally misinterpret (and then misrepresent) what you say, and the difficulties faced when seeking to communicate well at work are many and varied. Still, the best managers take many of those challenges in their stride because they intuitively understand that, when it comes to communication, how they say things is just as important as what it is they have to say in terms of making an impact. They know too that, when they communicate with others, be that one or many, the messages flying back and forth have two important elements – *content* and *context*. They understand that content relates to the words they choose, while context – the emotional part – is about how those words are transmitted and relates to tone and body language.

Content

Any number of problems can arise in relation to content, from using inappropriate language for the audience in question to overuse of meaningless jargon, such as all that 'going forward' and 'leveraging' gibberish. Recently, I was at a meeting discussing a potential problem when one of those sitting around the table suddenly chimed in that "we need to get *air cover* on this one" and the rest nodded in agreement, as if we were all sitting in a bunker in Afghanistan. I mean, spare me. Plain English, please. What is also worth highlighting on the content issue is how it takes some people so long to actually get the words out, or where others have a tendency to use 20 words when five would suffice. It's important to be clear, concise and get to the point in a timely fashion.

Context

Context includes your tone and body language and, as is widely known, all the research shows that this far outweighs the actual spoken word in terms of impact. Tone is often misused in communication situations, from those who don't speak loud enough to others who mistake shouting for power of argument. Raised tone can, of course, be appropriate on occasion to emphasise annoyance, or even just to get a word in when others believe in talking over you, but as a rule shouting detracts from your message, as people wonder why you are being so 'emotional' and in doing so likely miss the gist of what you have to say. Shouting also gives the impression that you lack self-control so for a variety of reasons, even when you are justifiably annoyed, a firm tone works best. Of course, the level of your voice is just one tonal issue, there are plenty more concerns, such as pace, pitch and pronunciation as well as being too curt or even too formal/informal depending upon the circumstances.

That said, it is essential to bring passion to the points you make – appropriate to the circumstances, naturally. Don't get me wrong, I am not talking about overdoing the emotion, but it's important to show real passion in your tone of voice in a way that is relevant to the topic and the audience. Put a bit of feeling into it.

With regard to body language, there are a multitude of potential sins. When transmitting messages your body language should always reinforce what you are saying, not detract from it; and especially in situations where you feel somewhat nervous or intimidated, you need to work hard to get things right.

All of us should constantly strive to enhance our ability to communicate, but we don't always give these basics the attention they deserve. This is partially down to the fact that communicating is seen as a natural activity, something that we learned to do when we were young and now that we've 'mastered' it, there's not much more to be done other than a bit of tweaking here and there. Unfortunately, what we don't always realise, or admit, is that as well as the good things we have learned, we have also developed bad communication habits along the way, about which we may not even be aware. Others are, however. And if you watch managers in action who are poor at getting their message across, it's usually fairly basic stuff that they are getting wrong. So, in conclusion here, you should never stop focusing on the nuts and bolts of how you communicate so that you are constantly developing and improving in this vital area.

2. Styles of Communication

As a manager, you will naturally be communicating with people in a variety of ways on a multitude of subjects, hopefully using different styles that are appropriate to the matter or scenario at hand. While this style issue is again not something that you probably give a whole lot of thought to, it's worth reflecting upon because how you use different styles of communication has a major impact on how effective you are as a communicator and as a manager. The diagram below shows the different styles that you can adopt to communicate with your team:

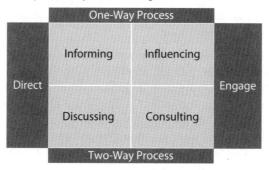

Generally, how you communicate can fluctuate from a **Direct** (informing and discussing) model to one where you seek to **Engage** (influencing and consulting) people in order to win them over to your ideas, and you can do so using one-way or two-way styles. These are all valid approaches and can be applied as follows:

In terms of the **Direct** Model:

- *Informing* At times being a manager means that you have to make decisions, or implement those taken by your superiors, which are not open to debate. In such circumstances you need to inform your people – and while you might let them blow off steam, or you will naturally explain the finer points of what's planned – there is really no point in getting into a detailed discussion with them about the matter because they simply have to accept that the decision has been made. It's out of their control.

A team briefing is another good example of where you might apply this style – it's largely one-way and you are informing them on work-related matters, or you might also use this style of communication when you need something to be done in a hurry.

Using the informing method is perfectly acceptable once you are not being aggressive in how you apply it, and if you don't think that informing equates to railroading, whereby you close down any discussion on the matter.

- *Discussing* If you only rely on the informing style all the time, which is essentially a one-way approach, then this becomes very limiting because your people need more input than that if you want them to fully engage. So, at times you need to adopt a 'discussing' style where people can explore issues in detail with you. You may not change, nor be in a position to change, decisions made, but you are at least prepared to discuss at length the views and concerns of employees about those decisions, and where possible tweak them in response. Again, this is a perfectly acceptable style in the right circumstances and meetings are a good example of where you would be deploying it.

In general, the **Direct** model of communication has its limitations in that, even where discussion is possible, by and large decisions have already been made and employees really don't have all that much input into them. To counterbalance this, on other occasions, rather than impose ideas and decisions on your people, you need to shift to an **Engage** approach to how you communicate and within that you can again apply two styles:

- *Influencing* Influencing is a one-way style which involves convincing others that an idea or decision is the right way to go. With this style, you use persuasive arguments to win people over. A good example of where you might use this approach is in trying to convince people that a change you are proposing is for the best – it's not the case that you are telling them this is how it will be, but rather the onus is on you to try to inspire and excite them about what you want to happen. This is such an important approach for today's manager that it is dealt with in greater detail below.

- *Consulting* A consulting style of communication is where you fully engage with your people to discuss issues, explore options and collectively agree on the best way forward. Some managers are uncomfortable with this style of communication as they fear they might lose control in such circumstances, or that things might get out of hand in some way.

While the four styles of communication outlined above are clearly not complicated, applying them in practice can be far more challenging. Naturally, the Direct styles are easier on you in the sense that they allow you to retain high levels of control over the interactions. However, the reality of the modern work-place is that the influencing and consulting styles of communication are far more prevalent now than they were even a decade ago, and all managers need to be comfortable using them.

Particularly, you should focus on your ability to influence and persuade others, because that's the style you will likely need to use more frequently in future. Think of it this way: in general terms, as alluded to earlier, employees are less willing to accept being told what to do all the time and that's now an established trend in the world of work. It's not going away. More pressingly, you will require greater flexibility from your people in the months and years ahead, and will want them to go beyond the call of duty on occasion, but you cannot force them to do any of those things. Equally, your superiors will be keeping a tight rein on budgets, so to get the resources you want will require you to make a strong case in support of your demands. All such instances will require you to influence and persuade others. It's also important to understand that your ability to do so is not really a separate set of skills at all – there are techniques of course such as how you frame and then make persuasive arguments – but your capacity for bringing others around to your point of view will be based upon a number of key factors:

- **Your ability to 'connect'** When seeking to persuade others it matters greatly whether you can truly connect with them. This is not to imply that you can only bring others around to your way of thinking if they like you, or feel a bond with you; nevertheless, changing opinions certainly becomes easier if the people you are trying to persuade (one or many) feel some form of connection with you. And you will connect with people on the following basis:
  ○ *Credibility* – you need to have credibility in the eyes of others if you hope to exert influence over them.
  ○ *Trust/Integrity* – if people don't trust you, or if you are seen to lack integrity, then you can forget about influencing them in a positive way.
  ○ *Passion and enthusiasm* – as touched upon earlier, without these qualities your ability to influence others is going to be severely restricted.
  ○ *Empathy* – unless you can put yourself in the shoes of others, you will find it very hard to develop arguments that respond to others' needs.

- **Your ability to build a compelling case** A basic assumption when seeking to influence others is that you can make a strong case which creates a win–win situation for both parties, or as close to that goal as you can achieve. In other words, you will rarely be able to give the other party everything they want or expect, but what you propose must meet their needs to some extent and not solely yours. In terms of framing a balanced case, consider the following points:
  ○ Be clear on who has the power to deliver what you want and who can put obstacles in your way.
  ○ Understand others' frames of mind and identify what needs your proposals can satisfy for them:
    What are their expectations and demands in relation to the issue at hand?
    What problems might you be able to solve for them with your offer?

What opportunities might arise for them if they follow your lead?

What are their likely objections and how might you respond to them?

- ○ Plan your pitch: in advance, think how to get their attention quickly, stimulate interest and how you will emphasise the benefits accruing from your proposals. Define those key outcomes in terms that will be meaningful for them – be specific not vague.

- **Your ability to make your argument** Of course, it goes without saying that having defined your case, you then need to make it in a way that really influences others and that challenge applies both in formal and informal settings. All the points made earlier about content and context of communication apply fully here too of course. Also, as you make your case:
  - ○ Engage people as you progress, build support as you go – don't wait until the end for a 'yes' or 'no' answer. For example, even getting people to agree that they are unhappy with the status quo shifts them a little in the direction you want them to go.
  - ○ Do not attempt to oversell your proposals – read the situation continuously and when you feel you have done enough, ask for their response. Make that call for action.
  - ○ Be ready for objections – listen to them when raised and address those concerns by offering tangible solutions.
  - ○ Clarify agreement and next steps before ending.

Research shows that, in general, people are strongly influenced by experts, or those who can show they deeply understand a particular subject. Therefore, when interacting with others, successful influencers tend to play up their knowledge levels regarding the matter at hand in order to increase their impact. Of course, the danger here is not to do so in a manner that is perceived as condescending by those you are seeking to win around; coming across as an arrogant know-it-all definitely won't help, so you always need to find the balance appropriate to your audience.

Given the changing dynamics of work today, you are called upon as a manager to influence your people far more often than someone in your position may have needed to do even 10 years ago, so it is something you should seek to master if you haven't already done so. Yes, it is harder to 'sell' than 'tell' but it's infinitely more productive in the long run.

The focus here has been on how to make yourself better understood by using various communication skills, styles and techniques to your advantage. Communication is such a vital part of what you do as a manager, and no matter how long in the tooth you are, there is always room for improvement. One thing is certain: if our château-owning friend had been a more effective communicator when dealing with his builders it is unlikely he would have ended up staring into a field of rubble shouting "This is not what I wanted!"

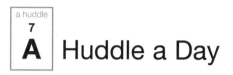

A | Huddle a Day

"Do you guys huddle every day?"
Blank stares all round.
"Cuddle, is it?" shouted out some smart aleck from down the back.
Cue giggling from some in the room.
"No, *ha-ha*, very funny – I said huddle!" answered the speaker, sounding somewhat exasperated. "Don't you guys huddle every day…?"

Not all jargon travels well. Or so I was reminded when speaking at an event. The audience, a group of mid-level managers, were attending a short workshop on 'Team Communication'. There were a number of speakers and the man before me was from the US. It was he who used the term 'huddle', which as you may know is an American Football term, where the team gets together in a close circle to plan the next play. He was referring to 'huddling' in a work context, which is well understood in the States no doubt. On this side of the Atlantic we usually refer to them as 'briefings'.

Terminology aside, I was amazed by the response when the group finally understood the question. Very few of them, in fact virtually none, held daily briefings with their teams. That's a lost opportunity, and briefings are potentially such an important contributor to team effectiveness that it's worth reflecting upon what's currently happening in this regard within your business.

In my experience, briefings are completely underused in organisations; they either don't happen at all, or are held intermittently, only when something major arises, or if a really special event is at hand. You should consider making the holding of a daily team briefing a 'non-negotiable' for all managers and supervisors in your business, including yourself, for they have many benefits, ranging from:

- Providing an opportunity for quick, concise communication on day-to-day work matters.
- Enabling the giving and receiving of feedback on a daily basis – so a manager can 'strike while the iron is hot' and deal with issues before they grow and get worse.
- Reinforcing the notion of 'team' when everybody comes together each day, and also implicitly making the point of who is in charge of it.
- Helping to gauge the 'mood' of employees and to identify if the team spirit is positive or not.
- Identifying if cliques are forming amongst employees simply by observing who stands with whom each day. It is also possible to get a sense of how a new hire is assimilating into the team.

- Helping to spot who the informal leaders are and whether they are playing positive or negative roles.
- Allowing managers to continuously reinforce the business vision and mission.
- Saving time, as a common message can be communicated to all at once rather than having to repeat the same thing to different individuals.

There are few things in business life which produce such valuable (and proven) returns as briefings for what is in reality a relatively small investment of time each day.

1. Making the Most of Briefings

In terms of getting the most from briefings, think about the following:
- *Pick a time and stick to it* It's important that briefings become a set part of the daily routine. Pick the most appropriate time to hold them and then keep to that consistently. Same time, same place, every day. Make it a habit.
- *Keep them short* Briefings – the clue is in the name – must never become meetings and they should focus on priorities/immediate concerns at hand. They are largely about providing direction, offering guidance and feedback to your people, listening generally to concerns and gauging team mood and dynamic. Where more in-depth issues arise, you should acknowledge the concerns raised and then agree to discuss them in detail at the next team meeting. Briefings should avoid all the pitfalls associated with meetings, being short and streamlined, no more than 10–15 minutes max. They must start and finish on time. They should not take people away from work, because they are held in the middle of the work area, or certainly close to it.
- *Stay standing* If everyone stands during briefings, this will contribute to maintaining focus and keeping things moving. When people sit, they tend to relax a little and often when tired they either tune out, or want to be able to stay sitting for as long as they can.
- *Structure briefings* Although they are generally informal, that doesn't mean preparation is not needed. Remember, in the space of a few minutes it's necessary to:

   Inform – give team members sufficient information to guide them for that day, or to update them on important matters.

   Involve – get their general views on matters at hand.

   Inspire – motivate and engage people.

None of the above can be achieved without some degree of preparation and a basic structure which keeps you on track, so:
- *Come Prepared* Before the briefing, take a couple of moments to gather and structure your thoughts. Be clear what needs to be said and know what input is wanted/needed from your team. Make sure not to be over-ambitious either in what can be covered within the allotted time.
- *Kick it off* Always try to begin in an upbeat way, without coming across as over-enthusiastic or too contrived in your approach: it's not the X-Factor after all so there's no need to fake things. Start off by outlining the key areas to be covered and encourage their participation. An important point to remember

here is that when general praise is due it's always a good idea to start the briefing with it, as it sets the scene in a nice way. That said, on days where there aren't a whole lot of positives to highlight, or when you have to raise concerns, it is best just to be upfront about whatever the problem is – not in a nasty, aggressive way, but simply letting people know what happened and what has to be done to put things right.

Over the period of a year, employees will see that when they do well, they will get positive feedback and when they don't, they will also be told in clear and unambiguous terms. In reality, by having this mix of good and bad feedback, delivered in the right way, the positive comments will actually have more impact when given.

- *Keep it flowing* Briefings should be vibrant affairs, with the relevant points covered without side-tracking. Take the lead in the briefing, working through the prepared points, soliciting input from the team as appropriate and ensuring that everyone is clear about what is required. However, there can be a fine line between allowing input from team members and a briefing turning into a meeting, and you may need to support your younger managers and supervisors when they first start to deliver briefings until they learn to get the balance right.

- *Wrap it up* Summarise what has been agreed and quickly make sure that all individuals are clear on whatever tasks or duties have been assigned to them. It is always important to end briefings on a positive note, and more so if negative feedback has been delivered.

Briefings may seem like a low-level concern, particularly if you are a seasoned manager, but I would wager that if you look around your business you will see that briefings are either not happening at all, or are not being used to best effect. Not holding a short briefing each day doesn't seem like such a big deal, and, on its own, it isn't. But a 10-minute briefing held every day would lead to around 2,500 minutes of communication within a team over a period of a year, or in other words 40+ hours! Multiply that by every team or department in your organisation and that's a lot of effective communication.

Can you afford to ignore those potential returns any longer?

I Was So Bored in There I Thought I Was Going to Die

"A meeting is an event at which the minutes are kept and the hours are lost."

I don't know who is responsible for that little quip, but it's a fairly accurate description of how we can all feel about meetings. Moving between organisations working on various projects, I am constantly surprised at just how frequently people are frustrated, or even angered, by what they view as having to attend too many meetings or, more likely, too many pointless meetings. It happens all the time in large and small businesses alike, in the public and private sectors, to the extent that moaning about meetings must be one of the most common pursuits in the world of work!

When you are in charge of others, regardless of where you sit in the hierarchy, then you will be responsible for managing meetings of some kind – the frequency and importance of which will naturally differ depending upon your seniority. Regardless of how often you run them, or how critical they are, a failure to manage those meetings for best effect not only damages your credibility but also impacts on the motivation and productivity of others too. Yet, for such an important activity undertaken by managers around the globe, meetings regularly fail and often for fairly common reasons.

Some of those common pitfalls include:

Attitude: Problems here can of course take many forms, but a major factor contributing to ineffective meetings is simply how some people view them. Often, individuals can adopt a casual approach, believing that it is acceptable to arrive unprepared, or late, and to contribute little whilst there. Unfortunately, such attitudes frequently go unchallenged, so that over time people become 'conditioned' that they are acceptable and the problems get worse, not better.

Linked to this is how some individuals view meetings as opportunities for game playing of various kinds. For example, an individual may have an issue with their boss, a colleague, or be disgruntled about work in some way, and meetings can provide them with a useful platform to act out their frustrations. Others can sit through meetings, pay lip-service to what has been agreed yet the minute they exit, they begin to work against any defined proposals. Again, this type of behaviour, when not challenged, tend to get worse over time.

Organisation and management problems: A multitude of difficulties can also occur in this category, from poorly planned and communicated meetings right up to poor time-management skills once they are underway. Even when a clear agenda has been agreed, if it's not managed correctly, people can wander off-topic or get bogged down on minor or irrelevant issues. A further concern that can be pinpointed in this area is how meetings can end up being a discussion by a few in attendance, whilst the majority have little or no input, or where there are side meetings going on within the meeting itself.

Impact concerns: Another common failing with meetings is that even when action is agreed between participants, there can often be little follow-up afterwards to ensure that any agreed action is implemented. In other words, nothing happens, and this in turn can reinforce negativity about future meetings.

These are some of the categories of problems that lead to ineffective meetings, and no doubt they will resonate with your own experience.

What seems to be overlooked, or at least underplayed, by many managers is the fact that there are substantial costs, financial and otherwise, attached to failed meetings; taking a group of employees, at any level, away from their work even for an hour costs money in terms of productivity and these costs are magnified when the meeting produces little of concrete value. On the hard cost side of things, let's imagine you have a regular weekly meeting with 10 attendees that runs for one hour. At an average salary of €30,000 per year, that translates roughly to €15 per hour per person, or €150, leading to a total cost for this one management meeting alone of €7,500 or so per annum; not an insignificant sum and particularly so these days when every penny counts. And if those meetings are unproductive, then a significant proportion of that cost is essentially money down the drain. And that's for one weekly meeting. Worse still are the hidden costs associated with the damage caused to motivation and morale to those who have to attend these meaningless or badly run events.

Here are some simple things you can do to run better meetings:

1. Prepare for the Meeting

There is not a manager in the world who would argue against the need to be fully prepared for a meeting, but how often have you seen the person who is hosting one arriving next to last, with a flustered look on his or her face letting you know that they are ill prepared – at least mentally – for what lies ahead? A not too infrequent occurrence, I would suggest. So, it's time to get the dusty record machine out, put the old and scratched 12-inch on the turntable, and play it over and over again until the message finally sinks in: when it comes to meetings, *failing to prepare is preparing to fail.*

In terms of preparation, you need to focus on the basics, such as:
- What is the purpose of the meeting?
- What do I want to achieve?
- Who actually needs to be there to achieve that goal?
- What is the most appropriate time to hold the meeting?
- Where is the best place to hold the meeting?

- What will be discussed – the agenda?
- And what can reasonably be covered in the time available?

The question to ask yourself is not whether you know what should be prepared in advance of a meeting, i.e. the above, but whether you actually do that preparation – every single time.

Another preparation consideration, beyond the logistics, is to recognise that when you host a meeting, you are the centre of attention and when you do it to a high standard – when others leave feeling their time has been well spent – then you raise your standing in their eyes and that naturally influences everything else you do as a manager. (The opposite is true also.) And what's more, when you do run effective meetings, people arrive to subsequent events with high expectations (and are usually well-prepared themselves) so naturally your meetings tend to go consistently well over time. On the other hand, when you mismanage your meetings, people don't prepare, come expecting to be bored out of their minds and tune out during it for as long as they can get away with.

2. Manage the Meeting

As with any successful mode of communication, meetings need some form of structure – they require a beginning, middle and an end. First and foremost, meetings should start on time. If you think about it, we often reward latecomers by waiting for them, or by rehashing everything once they finally arrive, which not only reinforces their bad behaviour but annoys those who did bother to arrive on time. Reward punctuality, not tardiness. Begin on the button and you will see the number of late arrivals dwindle over time. (A word in private will sort out any repeat offenders.)

It's clear that at the outset you also need to do things such as outline the agenda points, emphasise time constraints and allocate responsibilities, i.e. note-taker/ timekeeper. By the way, despite referring to them in the opening quote, the taking of *minutes* is not needed in most work situations; instead, record actions agreed, by whom they are to be implemented, and by when.

Often, and this might seem somewhat unusual, it can also be useful to appoint a 'conscience' at the beginning, one of those in attendance who is given permission to interject at any point during the proceedings when they feel things are going off-track. This can be a useful device to deploy as it gets another person involved in the running of the meeting, and it can come in handy for you when an off-agenda item is raised by someone: the conscience can step in and kill it, rather than you seeming to shut down debate on the matter. In general, the more people you can actively involve in different ways in managing the meeting the better as too many passengers around the table is never a good idea.

The main, or middle part of the meeting is about working through the agenda points, sticking to time, and getting (and recording) agreement on each point before moving to the next. Sounds easy, but, as you have no doubt experienced, this is where a multitude of problems can arise. The key here is how well you balance control and participation. Anyone can control a meeting by closing down discussion and stifling debate; this defeats the purpose, however. You want participation, but you also want to manage the discussion in a way that allows involvement from all participants, encourages healthy debate, discourages side-meetings and prevents conflict from getting out of hand. There's no magic answer as to how to get that balance right; it's about being assertive, using your communication skills for best effect, stepping in when you see unacceptable things happening, or when the 'heat' rises too much, and knowing when to wrap up the discussion on each point.

In terms of bringing meetings to a close, you should always endeavour to finish on time or, at the very least, that when the allocated period is reached you make a conscious decision to extend the meeting. Open-ended meetings are frustrating for all concerned and if you can't get through things in the agreed time, it's rare that you suddenly become hyper-productive by adding on a half-hour or so to proceedings. Unless it's a vital matter, it's probably best to stop and pick it up at the next meeting, or reschedule a get-together if it's more urgent. If you agree an hour for a meeting (which is about right for most run-of-the-mill work gatherings), then stick to it – and if you realise that you can't, then for the next time you should consider whether you are trying to do too much, or if you need to improve your meeting management skills.

To end the meeting, summarise all the points agreed, ensure that each attendee is clear about the action they must take afterwards – and the completion date for same – thank everyone for coming and for participating. It is also useful to get each person in attendance to vocally commit to what has been agreed – when people make 'public' commitments, they are less likely to renege later, or at least you will know by their tone that they are paying lip-service to something and you can then pick it up with them in private.

Lack of structure and poor management skills are the two most common causes of unproductive meetings. The ability to run a good meeting brings all of your communication and people management skills into play and you need to be 'in control' without seeming to be marshalling the event like a schoolteacher. You want to encourage participation, but only in a way that makes a positive contribution; allowing someone to drone on or stray off the point is not helpful. So, meetings are also about your ability to manage behaviour and your simple goal should be to make your meetings uplifting and inspiring affairs – not events that your people dread attending.

Recently, I was working in an organisation and as I passed a group of employees on the corridor – who had just left a meeting in one of the conference rooms – I heard one girl say "I was so bored in there I thought I was going to die" which was met with "*me too*" all round.

Would you really want your people saying things like that as they left one of your meetings?

Th e Important Thing is Not to Stop Questioning

In 1984, Bill Cosby approached ABC TV in the US seeking to pitch a new show about an upwardly mobile black family. ABC executives thought about it for a while but eventually turned him down. The rest is history, of course. Cosby later sold his idea – *The Cosby Show* – to NBC where it remained the number one show for four straight years, was a ratings winner for much longer, helped to lift NBC to first place nationwide and was the most profitable series ever made.

Every manager makes bad decisions from time to time, so missing out on one series, no matter how successful, is going to happen at some point to a TV executive. That said, poor management decision-making is a bigger problem than you might think across large and small businesses alike. In his important book, *Why Decisions Fail*,[14] Paul Nutt highlighted just how problematic it is by reporting on a study of nearly 400 business decisions made by senior managers in medium to large organisations which resulted in the alarming statistic that half the decisions made were not up to scratch because "either they were not able to withstand the uncertainty, conflict, or change common in the work environment, or they could not elicit the buy-in necessary to make them stick." This kind of indictment of managerial decision-making crops up in study after study; it's not an isolated finding, nor is it an exaggeration to say that many decisions fail in the workplace.

In Nutt's findings, the causes of the bad decisions included:
- The decision-making process itself was flawed; in addition, little analysis was undertaken as to the shortcomings within the process meaning that the same failures occurred time after time.
- Decision-makers based many decisions on prior commitments. In other words, they arrived at a conclusion first and the decision-making process was designed to justify that conclusion. Essentially, they put the cart before the horse.
- Decision-makers spent time and money on the wrong things, tasks that did not add value to making the best possible decision.[15]

---

[14] Nutt, *Why Decisions Fail: Avoiding the Blunders and Traps That Lead To Debacles*, (Berrett-Koehler 2002). Reprinted with permission of the publisher. © 2002 by Paul C. Nutt, Berrett-Koehler Publishers, Inc., San Francisco, CA. All rights reserved. www.bkconnection.com
[15] *Ibid.*

Given the importance of decision-making for any manager, this is an area of competence well worth reflecting upon. One commonly asked question here is what role does, or should, gut feeling play in decision-making? So, that's perhaps a good place to start.

1. Gut Feeling is Good ... or is it?

You may already know that, in the weeks and months immediately after the attacks of 9/11, air travel within the US fell by up to 20%, whereas road travel increased dramatically. People, out of fear, and perhaps as a result of the mass hysteria that understandably took over at that time, followed their gut instinct and chose not to fly. This was likely to be the safer option they assumed. As it happened, that wasn't accurate. Not by a long shot. Travelling long distances by car is infinitely more dangerous than covering the same distance by plane. All the statistics confirm this. What's more, Gerd Gigerenzer, a German expert on risk, later calculated that over 1,500 additional Americans died on US roads in the year after 9/11 than would normally be the case.[16] It turns out that the 'gut feeling' decision – avoid flying at all costs – was incorrect in this instance because it was largely driven by fear. Those who took the rational decision and believed that flying was actually likely to be safer than before, due to heightened security, turned out to have made the better choice.

To a greater or lesser degree, we all use gut feelings to support decision-making. And we all know too that we should not over-rely on it, especially when it is driven by irrational forces. Particularly in business life, depending solely on intuition can prove fatal. Still, we all have stories of decisions taken in the past which were based on instinct alone and that turned out to be great choices, so is there any guide to help us to decide when gut feeling is good?

Andrew Campbell and Jo Whitehead, directors of London's Ashridge Strategic Management Centre, writing in the *McKinsey Quarterly,* provide some guidance on this question.[17] The general thrust of their article is that we cannot prevent gut instinct from influencing our judgements, but what we need to do is to identify situations where it is likely to be biased and then strengthen the decision-making process to counterbalance the resulting risk. In other words, to protect decisions against bias, we first need to know when we can trust our gut feelings and be confident that they are drawing on appropriate experiences and emotions. According to Campbell and Whitehead, there are four questions or tests that can assist in this:

(a) Have You Experienced Similar (and Comparable) Situations Before?

They provide an example to illustrate this test. General Matthew Broderick, an official at the US Department of Homeland Security, made a decision on

[16] Gigerenzer, "Dread Risk, September 11, and Fatal Traffic Accidents" (2004) 15 (4) *Psychological Science*, pp. 286–287.
[17] Campbell and Whitehead, "How To Test Your Decision-Making Instincts" (2010) March *McKinsey Quarterly*. Adapted with permission. McKinsey & Company.

29 August 2005 to delay initiating the Federal response following Hurricane Katrina. He did so because he had previous experience of hurricanes and felt that it was worth waiting to see whether the levees had been breached and, as a result, how much danger people really faced in New Orleans. He felt that, as he was familiar with hurricanes in the past, he knew what he was doing.

Unfortunately, Broderick's previous experience with hurricanes was in cities above sea level. His delayed response, based on his gut instinct, proved disastrous because it did not result from analysing like-for-like experiences. Familiarity is important because our subconscious works on pattern recognition; if we have plenty of appropriate memories to scan, our judgement is likely to be sound, but they have to be comparable experiences.

(b) How Effective were Past Decisions Taken – Do You Know? Did You Get the Necessary Feedback?

Previous experience is useful to us but only if we have actually learned the right lessons. When we make a decision, our brains 'tag' it with a positive emotion – recording it as a good judgement. However, only subsequent feedback can verify whether it actually was or not. According to Campbell and Whitehead, the question is whether we always get that feedback. There are lots of reasons we may not. Perhaps we change positions, or even companies, before the outcomes of our decisions can be measured. We may simply move on without knowing, or checking; or, it might result from the fact that some managers have people around them – intentionally or otherwise – who filter the information they receive, or protect them from bad news so they might not actually get the feedback they need. As a result of such factors, we could continue to believe that a past decision was the correct one and naturally this feeds into future gut decisions we make.

(c) What are Your Emotional Triggers Associated with This Decision?

All memories come with emotional triggers, but some are more highly charged than others. A simple example was again used by Campbell and Whitehead in their article to highlight this key consideration. If a situation brings to mind highly charged emotions then these can unbalance our judgement. Knowing dogs can bite is very different from having had a traumatic childhood experience with dogs. The first will help you interact with dogs in a positive way: you always know to be a bit wary. The second can make you afraid of even the friendliest dog to the extent that you are frozen by irrational fears; this is similar to what happened in the case of the post 9/11 travel decisions mentioned above.

In terms of potential impact on decision-making, a second example here could be if you had been unfortunate enough to lose significant amounts of money on property investment in the past, and the emotional effect that would likely have on you. How might such a loss influence your 'gut' decisions in relation to any future property investment opportunities that were to arise?

(d) Do You Have any Inappropriate Personal Interests or Attachments Associated with this Decision?

When there is a personal connection to the outcomes of a decision then this has implications for whether we can trust our gut instinct. Campbell and Whitehead offer the following example. If you are trying to decide between two office locations for your company, one of which is much more personally convenient, you should be cautious, as your subconscious will have more positive emotional associations for the personally more appealing location than the alternative. It is for this reason that it is standard practice to ask those with self-interest in a particular decision to refrain from voting.

The authors' conclusion is that unless your gut decisions can pass all four tests then you need to strengthen the decision process to reduce the risk of a bad outcome. They also add:

> If we are to make better decisions, we need to be thoughtful both about why our gut instincts might let us down and what the best safeguard is in each situation. We should never ignore our gut. But we should know when to rely on it and when to safeguard against it.[18]

2. Improving How You Think about Issues

If you analyse your typical day, what opportunities do you have for 'thinking' time, in the sense that you can sit quietly and reflect at length upon an issue without disruption? Not a whole lot if you are like most managers. In fact, for many, the only meaningful time for reflection comes after the day's work is done, when they are tired and least primed for thinking effectively. So, the first thing you can do to improve your capacity for thinking is to actually make time and space for it.

A second step is to broaden how you think about matters at hand, and this can start when you involve others in the decision-making process. Too often we make decisions in isolation because it is quicker, or doing so enables us to retain control, but no single individual has the capacity to make all important decisions successfully on their own. Input from relevant parties is always valuable, and the bigger the problem, the more input needed.

When you are collectively exploring any problem or challenge, in terms of broadening the thought process, you need to try to take a more 'holistic' view of the matter. By nature we all have different ways of looking at issues: rational or emotional, optimistic versus pessimistic, unimaginative or creative. Added to that, certain individuals are more comfortable with facts and figures while others thrive on uncertainty and gut feeling. The trick when making decisions is to try to bring as many of these perspectives as possible into play, and this can be

---

[18] Campbell and Whitehead, "How To Test Your Decision-Making Instincts", (2010) March *McKinsey Quarterly*. Adapted with permission. McKinsey & Company.

achieved by using a variety of questions to stimulate your discussions and analysis.

Depending upon the specific issue, such questions might include:

Rational
- What do we know about this? Where's the evidence for that assumption?
- What has happened in the past when comparable decisions were made?
- What will this cost? What will the projected return be?
- Can we afford to do/not to do this?
- What might we have missed out on here?
- Do we have all the facts we need?

Positive/Negative
- What opportunities does this present us with? What other potential might arise?
- What benefits will this bring?
- How can we maximise those positive outcomes?
- Why can't/shouldn't we do this?
- What prevents us progressing on this? What's the downside?
- Why won't this work for us?
- What could happen if we get this decision wrong?

Emotional
- What's your gut feeling?
- How excited are you about this?
- What's scary about progressing with this?
- Why not just stick with the status quo?

Creative
- What other ways could we approach this?
- What's new in this area?
- If you had a blank sheet of paper, how would you design this?
- In a perfect world, how would the solution work?

This questioning approach encourages you to consider all angles associated with any potential decision of importance that you might take, and it doesn't require a genius to understand that individuals and teams that do take the broader view tend to make sounder and more resilient decisions than would otherwise be the case.

3. Have a Decision-Making Process

As with any important management activity, decision-making should be structured. Along with applying an approach such as the holistic questioning model above, your route map for making decisions should be clearly defined. The following framework is widely used:

- *Get to the real problem*
  - Focus on root causes not symptoms.
  - Be clear on what exact problem you are trying to solve.

- *Establish all the facts*
  - Explore the problem in detail; consult, investigate, research and analyse it from all sides until you have the full picture.

- *Consider all the options*
  - Identify a range of potential solutions; brainstorm all possibilities.

- *Evaluate the effects of each option*
  - Evaluate the advantages and disadvantages associated with each option, consider the likely short- and long-term implications, and prepare a cost-benefit analysis for each.
  - Identify the downsides for each alternative and how they might be mitigated.

- *Select and implement the best option*
  - Select the best option and plan its implementation.
  - Monitor progress and ensure that any blockages to implementation are dealt with effectively.
  - Measure impact.

You might not suddenly become a better decision-maker overnight, but you can increase your potential to do so. Making time for thinking, investing in it as a process and using tried and tested techniques, will help you, and your people, to broaden the parameters for how you examine given subjects; after all, considering all the constraints you operate under these days, every decision you take has to be a good one. And you don't have to be Einstein to understand what he meant when he said "The important thing is not to stop questioning. Curiosity has its own reason for existing."

A good starting point is to be curious about how you think and make decisions at present.

Hail the Fail

"Ever tried. Ever failed. No matter. Try Again. Fail again. Fail better."

Samuel Beckett

Success gets all the attention. There are no medals for coming last in the 100m sprint at the Olympics; no annual Oscar nominations for worst movie; no 'Bankrupt of the Year' ceremony; and employees don't get their picture on the wall for 'Incompetent of the Month'. No, it's all about achievement and it is normal that a success is more highly valued than a setback. But with so much failure, or at least the fear of it, in the air right now we all need to reflect a little upon our attitudes to the various knockbacks we encounter in life so that we can better respond to any we might face again. In doing so, I think the above words from Samuel Beckett have never been more relevant than in these difficult times, and so the focus for this Element is on failure; or, more precisely, on how you should deal with setbacks, whether they are your own, or those of your employees.

In addressing this issue, as you well know, not all failures are the same and I'll make the point early that when a setback results from someone being too lazy, or nonchalant about a given task, or if they simply couldn't be bothered about the outcome, then as their manager your response should be fairly straightforward: they cannot be allowed to underperform in that manner and you must use all your coaching and mentoring skills to ensure that they improve. (Topics covered in **Elements 14** and **15** will be useful in guiding you when faced with such issues.)

That said, failure can happen for other reasons too and some people, albeit often unintentionally, actually set themselves up to fail or lack the confidence to do what is required to succeed. Additionally, we can all fail on occasion even though we did our very best. So, managing failure is never a black and white issue and it's worth reflecting upon why and how some people fail and what you need to consider about this issue from a management perspective.

1. Understanding Self-handicapping

"I asked for it to be turned off before I went up there and it wasn't. I asked for it to be turned off at the break – it wasn't. The air conditioning doesn't affect Raymond because he throws a heavier dart and a very flat dart...".[19] This was Mervyn King, a darts player, blaming the air conditioning for his defeat to Raymond van Barneveld in the World Darts Championship semi-final. The organisers insisted that it had actually been switched off for the entire match.

[19] "The 10 Lamest Sporting Excuses", *Observer Sport Monthly*, 3 October 2004.

We all make excuses, at least to some extent, and they can be designed to justify poor performance of some kind. Yes, excuses are a fact of life and require little more thought than that. Or do they? Well, they may need more attention applied to them if the excuse-making turns into a form of *self-handicapping*. What on earth is that, you may be wondering? Well, here's some background on the concept.

In the 1950s, David McClelland, a Professor of Psychology at Harvard University, uncovered something interesting. He undertook a series of experiments based on the 'Ring Toss'[20] garden game, where you attempt to throw little plastic rings onto a peg. The children who participated in the research were first tested on their 'desire to succeed' or their 'need for achievement', then prior to throwing their first ring were told they could throw the rings from as close to, or as far away from, the peg as they wished. McClelland found that the children who were rated as having the highest achievement scores usually initially stood at a moderate distance from the peg which meant they had a challenging throw but one that was achievable. As they got better at the game, they extended their distance.

However, those with the lowest desire for achievement scores tended to do two things: either they got so close to the peg that they couldn't miss, or they stood so far back that they had little hope of making it. It was this last set of behaviours that McClelland found most intriguing – some children were essentially creating a situation where they would likely fail. But having stood so far back, they were protecting themselves, in that they had the 'excuse' that they couldn't have been expected to succeed from that distance. This notion of creating excuses to explain why we're not responsible for our mistakes, failures, or poor performance has been well researched in the past 50 years or so and is now widely known as 'self-handicapping' and is described as "an action or choice which prevents a person from being responsible for failure."[21] In order words, we do or say something which will help us justify a setback of some kind in order to save face or protect our self-esteem. And there are two types of self-handicapping.

The first is known as *behavioural* self-handicapping, and this is where we, as the children above did, make a task harder for ourselves to protect our self-esteem in case we fail. In essence, we place barriers in our way, or set ourselves up for failure. One example of this can be when we define totally unrealistic personal or work-related goals – we raise the bar so high that we can later console ourselves that it was simply too ambitious in the first place.

The second form is called *claimed* self-handicapping, and it's where we contrive an obstacle to our performance. For example, if I am very nervous about making a presentation, I might spend time telling all and sundry beforehand that I had been sick the previous night and am not ready for the talk – laying the

---

[20] McClelland, *The Achieving Society* (2nd edition, Martino Fine Books 2010).
[21] Kolditz and Arkin, "An Impression Management Interpretation of the Self-Handicapping Strategy" (1982) 43(3) *Journal of Personality and Social Psychology*, pp. 492–502.

ground for failure. Or I might blame the air conditioning, as our dart-throwing friend did.

Self-handicapping is of course a very complex area and the above represents but a snapshot of what's involved; however, research shows that everyone self-handicaps to some degree, and it's to be found in all walks of life. Naturally, sometimes excuses are valid, and therefore not all excuse-making is self-handicapping; it's more a question of frequency and intent. When you watch people closely on this issue, you will likely find that for a few individuals there is always a justification, or a barrier of one sort or another. So, why as a manager should you be interested in this issue of self-handicapping?

Well, first off, you should consider whether you have a propensity for any form of self-handicapping, beyond the normal valid excuses that we all have from time to time. You may also need to ask those you know and trust in a work context for their views on this matter to get the true picture. Is self-handicapping a frequent occurrence for you? Is it holding you back? Secondly, consider what some of your employees might be doing in this regard. Are there issues with unrealistic goal-setting, fear of failure and so on that are causing individuals to self-handicap? How is that affecting their performance? Is it having an impact on other team members? In short, even though such actions might be unintentional, you need to identify and resolve behaviours that lead to people underperforming or seeking to justify failure.

2. Coping with Failure

Of course, sometimes, despite our very best efforts, we fail. When we have put our heart and soul into something and still come up short, then that is nothing to be ashamed of. When faced with such circumstances, as a manager, you should consider how you personally cope with setbacks and how you might help others to do so.

To begin with, failure can actually be a good thing. This is true when you do your best and still miss out, but learn from the experience and develop as a result. The reality for most of us, though, is that we feel embarrassed or ashamed when we don't achieve what we wanted or expected – call it what you will, it still feels like a failure. And often the shame of failure can be worse than the failure itself, can't it? But it is precisely such emotional responses which prevent us from learning the lessons and moving on.

So, what might you do to better cope with such setbacks? Here are some points to consider:

- *Try to manage the emotion* Failure – perceived and real – hurts. It damages the ego, chips away at our self-esteem and erodes our sense of self-worth. But if you allow those negative emotions to take root, not only could you miss out on any lessons to be learned from the experience, you are likely to damage your ability to pick yourself up and try again in future. Of course, it's not easy to simply ignore the emotions associated with our failures, but it is possible to manage them – at least to the point where you control them, not they you.

It can be good to be angry with yourself, to feel frustrated, even to feel guilt or shame; it shows you care, are ambitious and want to do better. It is not good, however, when you allow such feelings to run riot to the extent where you turn inwards and begin to undermine your confidence and drive. Such responses are corrosive and always self-defeating. When faced with major setbacks, it is important to keep things in perspective and stay positive.

- *Try to reframe the failure* One way to try to benefit from a setback is to consider how it might be reframed. For instance, it is well known that Thomas Edison had many failures before he invented the light bulb. But each and every one of those dead-ends brought him closer to his ultimate goal. Given the scale and number of his setbacks, many would have thrown in the towel, but Edison reframed it: "I have not failed, I've just found 10,000 ways that won't work." With time and distance from the event, you too can begin to better frame a supposed failure. There is always more than one way to look at an incident.

- *Try to pinpoint the lessons* It's very easy to say "pinpoint the lessons", but it's harder to identify what they may be. And naturally the lessons to be learned depend upon the nature and scale of the setback involved. That said, regardless of what has happened, there is always at least one lesson to stem from any failure and that is, by coming through it, you have developed your mental toughness and resilience – at least to some extent – which can help you in future. Learning how to cope with a setback is always a valuable lesson.

For all of us, any important setback should trigger a reassessment of our abilities and potential. Not, as highlighted, in a negative, self-critical fashion, but in an honest, objective and rational way. From that, we may identify skills or knowledge gaps to be addressed. Or, maybe a more radical rethink of where we are headed is required given our abilities and levels of motivation.

To close, failures come in many guises, from pure laziness or disinterest, to the self-handicapping variety, right across the spectrum to setbacks which come even though we did our best. Each of these requires a different response, both in terms of dealing with your own failures and in helping your employees to cope with theirs. When a setback does come despite everyone's best efforts, the important point to remember, and to communicate to others, is that those who fail having given their all are in good company. I could list page after page of quotations from successful people, describing the contribution that failures have made to their ultimate success, but one anecdote about J.K. Rowling, author of the Harry Potter books, does the trick.

During an address to the Harvard Alumni Association, Rowling spoke to the audience about failure and, as part of that, related her own personal story about how, as a young woman, she had given up her dream of writing novels to study something more practical. Despite that, she explained, she still ended up as an unemployed single mother "as poor as it is possible to be in modern Britain without being homeless". But during that difficult period, she realised that she still had a wonderful daughter, an old typewriter, and an idea: "You might never fail on the scale I did," Rowling told the audience. "But it is impossible to live without failing at something, unless you live so cautiously that you might as well not have lived at all, in which case, you fail by default. You will never truly know yourself, or the strength of your relationships, until both have been tested by adversity. Such knowledge is a true gift, for it is painfully won, and it has been worth more to me than any qualification I ever earned."

About out

employees

Think about how
to get the most
from your people

Managers are from Mars

"I think the challenge for some managers is not to bring out the best in their employees, instead, they ought to stop bringing out the worst in them." The speaker left those words hanging in the air, waiting for a reaction. As he did so, I looked at the faces of one or two around me. This latest onslaught, in what had been an overtly confrontational talk, wasn't going down at all well with a couple of the assembled managers in the room. But the speaker wasn't finished. "If some managers cared half as much about people as they did about numbers, then work life would be a hell of a lot better for all concerned", he continued. At that point, a man in the front row seemed to have had enough and he was quickly joined in the 'discussion' by a few more red-faced participants. Things got a little heated to say the least.

This incident happened at a seminar I once attended, and while the speaker was trying to make a valid point – that being how some managers need to pay more attention to the relationship they have with their employees – his in-your-face style didn't work for some in attendance, and as such the message was mostly lost on them. Still, the event set me thinking about the importance of the manager–employee relationship in general and how, as with any relationship, there can be a whole host of misunderstandings and differing perspectives which can cause problems.

It should come as no shock that the relationship between you and your staff is an important one, but just how vital it is can often be overlooked. A study led by Brad Gilbreath,[22] an Associate Professor at Indiana University-Purdue University and reported in *Psychology Today*[23] emphasised just how important the manager-employee relationship actually is. He found that:

> A worker's relationship with the boss was almost equal to his relationship with his spouse when it comes to the impact on his well-being. A rewarding job or even good relationships with co-workers cannot compensate for a negative relationship with the boss.[24]

Surprised? You shouldn't be when you consider that you directly influence the pattern of your team members' lives for over 2,000 hours in any given year. At least they get to choose their partners; they're landed with you!

[22] Gilbreath and Benson, "The Contribution Of Supervisor Behaviour To Employee Psychological Well-Being" (2004) 18 *Work & Stress*, pp. 255–266.
[23] Lawson, "Good Boss, Bad Boss" *Psychology Today*, 1 November 2005.
[24] *Ibid.*

1. Differing Perspectives

Given the significance of the relationship, the way in which managers and employees view various aspects of work-life really does matter, and there is plenty of research available to show that perceptions are often very different. I have seen countless examples of these opposing views in action over the years, and one particular case sticks in my mind due to the sheer scale of the perceptions gap.

The company in question was a big player in the aviation sector with global operations but one which had a history of poor 'industrial relations', as was the favoured term at the time, in its UK and Irish division in particular. I was part of a team drafted in to examine the issues and propose solutions. One of the first tasks we undertook was to have managers and employees complete a short organisation climate survey which was based on important issues such as communication, trust, common purpose, etc. The results were truly astounding. The collated findings from the management team, when compared against those of the employees were, for the most part, entirely conflicting. Whereas managers, perhaps unsurprisingly, rated things like the quality of communication as being excellent, employees saw it as extremely poor. The only area where the ratings matched was that all believed trust was non-existent, which was indeed accurate. When we brought the two 'sides' together (another telling phrase they used in the company) and showed them the results for the first time, the room erupted into laughter as the realisation dawned on all concerned just how different their respective views really were. Resolving the issues took many years but the shock behind the laughter in the room that day was undoubtedly a turning point.

Sure, this may have been an extreme case, but my experience tells me that in all businesses there are at times significant differences in perceptions, to the extent that you would be forgiven for thinking that some managers and employees come from different planets.

2. Misunderstanding the Motivators

This mismatch in management–employee viewpoints is particularly concerning when it relates to specific work issues such as motivation. A study by two researchers from Harvard[25] showed just how different perceptions can be on the issue of motivation. They surveyed more than 600 managers from a variety of companies asking them to rank the impact on employee motivation and emotions of five workplace factors commonly considered significant:
- Interpersonal support
- Recognition
- Incentives
- Support for making progress
- Clear goals

'Recognition' topped the list of the surveyed managers when asked what they felt most motivated their people. While that makes sense, they were wide of the

[25] Amabile and Kramer, "What Really Motivates Workers" (2010) January, *Harvard Business Review*, pp. 44–45.

mark as it turned out. The researchers also tracked the day-to-day motivation levels of hundreds of employees and they found that their top motivator was actually 'Making Progress' (which incidentally was the lowest ranked issue by the managers). The study showed that three-quarters of employees felt most highly motivated, not when they were recognised, but on days when they felt they were making progress.

Now, whether you agree or disagree with these specific findings is not the key point here. The real issue is that with such differing perspectives on what actually motivates employees, you might be doing things in your business that you believe will make a difference when in fact such issues may not be all that important for your people. Or, maybe you are doing the right things, just not enough of them. Here's a non-scientific example of how good intentions can go awry.

I was recently chatting to the owner of a business with about 20 employees. Like everyone else, they have had a tough few years, but some time back the company won a number of contracts that more or less secured the medium-term future. As a reward for their hard work and to thank them for their contribution, the owner explained how he and his management team decided to hold a night out for staff.

The event, however, caused a fair few unexpected problems. For starters, it was 'employees only', with no partners or spouses allowed, and this led to complaints. It was held on a week night, which meant that the younger crowd loved it but the older, married types felt it was an imposition on their evening and family time. As he recounted the general unhappiness surrounding the event, the owner was clearly frustrated that his efforts to do the right thing had resulted in more hassle and grief than had he done nothing at all. In fact, he told me that one older employee had even said to him after the event: "Who wants to go out on a Thursday night and be reminded what it was like to be young?"

On occasion, managers can unintentionally demotivate employees because they assume they know what motivates them. Evidence of this mismatch between what managers think and what people want is to be found everywhere, and the negative impact it has on motivation levels is not insignificant. For example, another Harvard study[26] made the not-too-surprising discovery that people are generally highly enthusiastic and motivated when they start a new job. However, based on their surveys of about 1.2 million employees, the researchers also found that in about 85% of companies employee morale declined sharply after their first six months and continued to deteriorate for years afterward. And what were managers doing 'wrong'? The authors of the study concluded that "there are several ways that management unwittingly demotivates employees and diminishes, if not outright destroys, their enthusiasm." This included factors such as:

[26] Sirota, Mischkind *et al.,* "Why Your Employees Are Losing Motivation" (2006) 11 *Harvard Management Update.*

- Clearly, reward and recognition are always important motivators for employees, even if they are not placed on top of the list every time, and this particular study found that about half the workers felt they received little recognition or credit, and two-thirds felt they were criticised more than praised.
- Another issue raised in the study – and this is again related to the 'Making Progress' finding above – is how some managers inadvertently make it difficult for employees to do their jobs by imposing too many procedures or hurdles to getting things done: creating an unwieldy bureaucracy, demanding too much paperwork and cross-checking, indulging in bad communication, etc. which all lead to frustration.
- They also make the point that "Many companies treat employees as disposable. At the first sign of business difficulty, employees – who are usually routinely referred to as 'our greatest asset'– become expendable."[27]

Could you inadvertently be doing things to put a damper on your employees' motivation levels?

3. Releasing the Reins to See the Gains

Another area where the mismatch in perceptions between managers and staff can come into play is with regard to the issue of empowerment. In 2008 and 2009, I conducted a comprehensive survey of Executive MBA participants at ESCP Europe in Paris, a leading European business school. Over 220 participated in the wide-ranging study, and these mid-career managers represented a broad mix of nationalities and industry fields. One section of the study asked participants to identify the things that bothered them most about the way they were managed by their superiors. The top 10 were:

1. Micromanaging
2. Not involving them in decision-making
3. Disrespecting them
4. Not providing freedom/autonomy
5. Not giving constructive feedback
6. Not recognising effort
7. Not communicating effectively
8. Not having, or communicating, an overall vision
9. Creating negativity or poor team spirit
10. Ineffective performance/failure to get things done

This list is not unusual in my experience, working with employees at all levels I see similar points cropping up time and time again. When you group these 10 concerns together by theme you find that people generally want to be involved and included, to feel valued and respected but at the same time they do not want to have their hands held too tightly. In particular, the issue of being micromanaged crops up repeatedly these days and employees, or certainly the better ones, generally crave more autonomy in their work lives and want to be empowered.

[27] *Ibid.*

Few would argue that the idea of empowering employees has merit, yet there is often a lack of appreciation of what that actually means, and the definitions available are as varied as they are numerous. So, here is probably a good place to attempt to define it in practical terms. First, empowering people forms an integral part of your wider efforts to engage employees and, as you are probably already aware, it means that you release the reins of control to allow them a greater degree of freedom over how they do their work as well as involving them more in decision-making about matters that impact upon them. Empowerment should be seen as a progressive activity, with a spectrum of options, which at one end of the scale can involve low-level empowerment, for example when you allow your people to make on-the-spot decisions within certain parameters. This kind of empowerment is good of course, but it only represents the tip of the iceberg when it comes to the extent of options available to you to empower your team.

True empowerment means working towards a goal where employees become genuine partners in the running of your business. It involves them in decision-making and allows them to take greater ownership of the way they plan and do their work. You may never reach that lofty objective, for many reasons, but over time you should work towards achieving high-level empowerment. And this is where the mismatch of perceptions can kick in on this issue: some managers believe they have fully empowered their people but are really only doing so at a very low level.

The points covered here about the discrepancy that can exist between managers and employees generally, as well as those in relation to specific issues such as motivation and empowerment, are worth reflecting upon and you should examine what problems in these areas might be prevalent in your business or department at present because the last thing you need right now are difficulties of that sort. The potential for mismatch is not solely confined to the areas covered here, so take a broad look at this issue. As a result, and no matter how many people you are responsible for, it's worth asking yourself some important questions in this regard:
- Do you really understand your people? Do you know what makes them tick – individually and collectively? And do they understand you?
- Are you consistently striving to deliver on those expectations in a way that is good for the employees and for the business?
- Might you unintentionally be doing things that are holding them back or serving to demotivate your people? Are there existing misperceptions that you could eradicate through better communication?
- What is the level of empowerment in your business at present? Does it run deep enough to the point that employees have real autonomy to make independent decisions on matters that relate to their jobs?

Finally, does it feel as if you are on the same planet as your employees most of the time?

Keeping the Bad Apples Out

According to a report on the CBS news website in the US, EmmaLee Bauer, a sales coordinator at a Sheraton hotel in Iowa, wasn't what you might call a highly motivated individual. Bauer seemed to have a lot of free time on her hands, so to look busy she began recording her working day in a journal. Her 'work' included typing observations such as: "This typing thing seems to be doing the trick. It just looks like I am hard at work on something very important", as well as other gems, like "I am only here for the money and, lately, for the printer access. I haven't really accomplished anything in a long while … and I am still getting paid more than I ever have at a job before, with less to do than I have ever had before. It's actually quite nice when I think of it that way. I can shop online, play games and read message boards and still get paid for it."[28]

Unfortunately for Bauer, committing such thoughts to paper (or more accurately her work computer), is always a risky venture and so it proved as her boss soon discovered the journal and promptly fired her. She was later denied unemployment benefits by a judge who said her journal showed a refusal to work and "amusement at getting away with it". You have to admire her audacity though for taking the case in the first place.

Thankfully, the majority of employees are honest, hard-working individuals. Everyone has off-days, but the bulk of people I encounter actually like their job and want to do it to the best of their ability. That said, some people either don't fit in, or fail to rise to expectations for various reasons and then there are those, albeit a very tiny minority, who consistently fall well below expectations. From experience you will already be well aware of this fact and the question, and focus here, is how do these various under-performers, from the mild to the severe, sneak under the recruitment radar with such apparent ease and frequency?

It is partially explained by the fact that there are individuals out there who thrive in an interview setting to the extent that they can pull the wool over our eyes. However, from what I have seen, the main reason why managers are so frequently caught out in terms of hiring people who later disappoint has more to do with the fact that the recruitment process itself is frequently mismanaged. This may sound harsh, but it is a reality, and particularly so where small or medium enterprises are concerned. Although there has been a vast improvement in the quality of recruitment practice and methods over the past decade or

---

[28] "Laziness Journal Costs Worker Her Benefits" CBS News, 11 February 2009. See http://www.cbsnews.com/2100-201_162-2377062.html

more, it's still far from a perfect process in many organisations. Given the risks and costs associated with poor recruitment, this is not something that can be ignored any longer.

1. Failures of Recruitment

Effective recruitment involves a comprehensive process, as shown in **Figure 12.1**, with many interlinked steps. Of course, the primary goal of the process should be to attract a pool of suitable candidates for any given post and then to ensure that you get the best of what's available. And that's how you should approach recruitment: positively, as a quest to find people who best fit with your organisation and the role to be filled. However, you also have to remember that it's a process intended to keep undesirable employees out too. You need to do everything in your power to minimise the potential for 'bad apples' to slip through the net.

Figure 12.1 **Overview of the Recruitment Process**

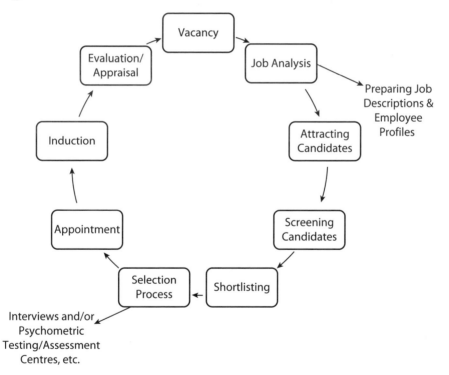

Even if all these steps are managed to perfection, you will still get caught out occasionally – it is a human activity after all – but just less often. The intention here is not to focus on all elements of this process, but rather to concentrate on the aspect of it that is likely to be of most relevance to you, namely the **interview** phase. You will no doubt be frequently involved in interviewing for new hires, at various levels, and even if you are very experienced in this area there is always room for improvement. In fact, studies have shown that, while veteran interviewers tend to believe they are good at selecting the right candidate, that level of confidence is often unfounded; experience is, after all, only of value if you have been doing the right things.

An important reason why some managers make poor selection decisions following interviews is that their focus is still too much on what someone can *do* – their skills and competences, as opposed to who they *are* – their personal qualities. Of course, a balance between both facets is evidently needed, but sometimes there is too much emphasis placed during the interview on exploring the doing bit at the expense of delving into the candidate's personality. However, when you think about it, you can quite easily determine what skills someone has from their CV, so the focus in terms of recruitment, and especially during the interview phase, should be to figure out whether a candidate is the right fit for your organisation. Ultimately skills can be learned, but it is far harder, I find, to change someone's personality, so you should use the interview to understand, as best you can, what type of person you are really dealing with.

In seeking to recruit any new employee, you therefore need to consider both *what* they can do and *who* they are. In relation to the latter, it is only through having a clear picture in your mind of the type of person you are looking for that you can ever hope to have any chance of finding the most suitable individual from the pool available. Many businesses today have developed employee profiles that help to pinpoint a range of traits and characteristics associated with key positions in the organisation, and if you don't currently have such tools, then ask yourself: on what basis are people being hired for various posts in your company at present?

Armed with a clear image of the ideal candidate, you can then more usefully prepare for interviews by devising a set of questions (and exercises if appropriate) based on that profile, which will help you to better know the person sitting in front of you. What's more, by using a simple weighted evaluation form – also based on the profile – each candidate can then be benchmarked against the ideal characteristics required.

2. Pitfalls Associated with Interviews

Dr Allen Huffcutt of Bradley University has identified seven principles[29] for getting the most out of recruitment interviews:

Principle 1: Acknowledge the Inherent Difficulty of Making Judgments from an Interview

It is easy to forget that an interview is at best a flawed mechanism for selecting individuals for employment. There are so many variables that even small imperfections in the process can lead to poor selection. In recognising those limitations you should therefore pay close attention to how you prepare for, and manage, interviews in order to ensure that you at least maximise their potential for success.

[29] Huffcutt, "From Science to Practice: Seven Principles for Conducting Employment Interviews" (2010) 12 *Applied H.R.M. Research*, pp. 121–136.

Principle 2: Know as Little About the Candidate as Possible

This is interesting, as it goes completely against the commonly held wisdom that you should know as much about a candidate before the interview. The reason Huffcutt promotes this view is that when an interviewer reviews candidate information beforehand, this can result in a three-step process coming into play:

1. First, when the interviewer reviews information in advance he or she forms a general impression of a candidate (and given that we are all human, we can be swayed by factors such as one candidate going to a particular school or university).

2. During the interview, when the interviewer has already formed a favourable impression of a particular candidate in advance, they can subconsciously shift from objectively probing and testing their suitability into an 'impression confirming mode', whereby they assess the answers of favoured candidates less harshly than others. This is known as the 'Halo Effect'.

3. Finally, the combination of the initial favourable impression and the selective testing of suitability during the interview can then carry through to the evaluation stage, whereby the applicant is given a higher rating than is perhaps justified. Think of it this way: if you have (subconsciously) made up your mind from the outset that this candidate outshines others, even when they don't, you will likely give them a higher score at the end in order to position them above the next best applicant.

In corresponding with Dr Huffcutt while preparing this piece, he made the very valid point that "it is important to note that the above process works in the negative direction as well. If an interviewer forms a negative impression of a candidate beforehand (e.g. the candidate went to a 'lesser' school), the interviewer can shift into an impression confirming mode and looks for things that confirm their negative impression. That of course can easily lead to asking more difficult questions, being more picky and ignoring or minimizing positive information."

This is a principle well worth reflecting upon and although you might still review candidate information in advance, you should try to avoid forming too favourable or unfavourable an impression beforehand.

Principle 3: Avoid Poor Questions

Ensure that your questions are planned in advance and based upon the job requirements and personal characteristics you are looking for. Allen Huffcutt suggests that "every question should relate directly to the knowledge, skills, abilities, and other characteristics ('KSAOs') associated with a given position". This is common sense perhaps, but when you watch unprepared interviewers in action, you quite often hear them asking questions that add little or no value to the decision-making process in terms of identifying candidate suitability. An example of this may well be where an interviewer, who perhaps hasn't had the time, or made the effort, to review the CV in advance, devotes an inordinate proportion of the interview asking the candidate to recount his or her past work experience, without really probing the value or learning from those positions or roles. Questions which allow the candidate to simply list off what they did previously in response are of little help in determining suitability.

Huffcutt also promotes the use of behavioural ("Tell me how you managed your team during an important project...") and situational ("What would you do if...") type questions to better understand candidates. It is also important, he emphasises, to avoid using the same-old formulaic questions for which candidates can offer pre-prepared answers, e.g. where do you want to be in five years?

Principle 4: Utilise Interview Structure

According to Huffcutt: "Of all the findings in the interview research literature, perhaps the most consistent and practically meaningful is the effect of structure."[30] In short, based on his analysis of a variety of research, the more structured the interview process, the more valid it becomes in terms of objectively assessing candidate suitability. Unfortunately, many managers still run poorly structured interviews that differ wildly between candidates in terms of length of time taken, the questions asked, and the degree of probing, thus making like-for-like comparisons between all candidates virtually impossible afterwards.

Principle 5: Avoid Making Judgements Early in the Interview

This is a well-known drawback with interviewing and there is no easy answer to overcoming our propensity to form early first impressions. However, as Huffcutt explains it is important to acknowledge that this is a pitfall, and then to work hard to delay one's decisions, which is a skill that can be developed over time. He concludes: "Like most skills, learning to delay judgements takes time and practice. It might be useful for interviewers to think of themselves as 'investigative agents', ones who do not arrive at a conclusion and take action until every nook and cranny has been explored."

Principle 6: Watch for Applicant Performance Effects

It is also well-known that some candidates can use various tactics during the interview that are designed to increase their standing, such as praising you personally, or the company, overstating their achievements and even downright fabrication. One would imagine that interviewers would see right through this type of thing, but Huffcutt's analysis of research on this particular area showed that "the use of these tactics by applicants can have a significant influence on the outcome of the interview".

Principle 7: Look for Multiple Sources of Evidence

The essential point here is not to over-rely on one interview, or single interviewers, as the primary selection method and even within interviews answers should be probed and tested rather than taken at face value. In addition, many companies use multiple interviews to better understand the individual. Beyond interviewing,

---

[30] *Ibid.*

the use of psychometric testing, assessment centres, presentations, reference-checking, etc. provide additional data to support decision-making.

While these principles are not necessarily new, given the extensive analysis of available research on interviewing undertaken by Allen Huffcutt, his views are certainly worth considering.

3. Making the Most of Interviews

Having identified some common pitfalls with interviews, the intention is not to go step-by-step through the interview process, as you will likely have had some form of training on this area. If you haven't, then you should definitely consider getting some because every new person you bring into your team has the potential to make it better, or a lot worse – the consequences of poor interviewing skills can be long-lasting. Rather, this section explores some points relating to the structure of the interview and the technique you use.

Before getting to those specific aspects of interviews, consider the following general tips on preparation, which may seem simple, but it's amazing how often they are still overlooked:

- *Always prepare fully for interviews in advance* As touched on earlier, you will often see an unprepared interviewer reading through a CV for the first time during the interview. This is particularly bad practice, so don't do it. Review the CV or application before the interview, but (as discussed above) be aware of any issues or factors that might sway you.
- *Prepare the interview area* Choose a private setting, not too formal, where you and the candidate can both concentrate. Holding an interview in your office is not ideal for many reasons, including that it's your 'turf', which means that you are going to be more relaxed in that environment and the candidate is likely to feel under greater pressure. It is also the place where you will potentially face most distractions that can disrupt the interaction. Don't underestimate the importance of the location you choose in terms of providing the right environment to bring the best out of the candidate and afford you the greatest opportunity to concentrate.
- *Prepare an interview plan* Incorporate into your plan the structured questions you develop based on the profile of the ideal candidate, and on the requirements of the job.
- *Limit the number of candidates* Try to limit the number you see in any one day so that you stay fresh and alert for all candidates.

With these preparation tips in mind, when holding the interview, there are many different interview structures that can be followed but as we have done for all communication scenarios in this book, let's keep things relatively straightforward and examine the interview in terms of three phases: beginning, middle and end.

The Beginning

Clearly, at the beginning of the interview, there are certain things you need to do. To start with, it is good practice to meet the candidate at reception personally and escort them to the interview room, as you can learn a lot about someone in those few minutes – their level of confidence, how at ease they are with small talk, and so on. Sometimes, as soon as a candidate enters the interview room, they can slip into 'interview mode' so on the walk up you can often get glimpses of the candidate's true self.

To kick off an interview you will of course want to put the applicant at ease, and to let them know how the interview will be structured, whether it's part of a wider process and so on. A relaxed candidate will perform better.

The Middle

The bulk of the interview should be devoted to finding out about the candidate. That sounds obvious, but the reality in many interviews is that the interviewer does too much talking; work through your questions and let the candidate speak. Apply the 80/20 rule: the candidate should talk for 80% of the time. That obviously does not mean you let them ramble on incessantly, you should probe and test (but not interrogate) their responses to get behind what are often rehearsed answers of one kind or another. As a rule you should:

- Begin with general questions moving to the more specific.
- Use your question technique to explore background, attitudes, suitability, etc. relevant to the job description and, more importantly, to the employee profile you are seeking.
- Use a variety of behavioural and situational questions relevant to the role.
- Follow your interview plan, and do so as closely as possible for all candidates asking them the same or similar questions. It is only through this approach that you can actually evaluate suitability against a common standard.

In terms of timing, this exploration phase of the interview should clearly form the main component. The general question also arises as to how long an interview should be and it's very difficult to suggest a set time but, in reality, for any position, interviewing for less than 30 minutes is not advised – and if you find you have candidates who are ruled out very early in the interview, then you might need to look more closely at the effectiveness of your screening process. As a rule, interview fewer candidates, for longer. For any management position, you should be looking at a first interview lasting up to one hour, and having a couple of interviews as part of the process.

Also keep in mind that as you assess the candidate they are also making judgments about you and the organisation, so you need to come across as professional – after all, you want the person you do select in the end to have a positive view of you when they turn up on day one.

The End

Once you have obtained all the relevant information you need, you should then allow the candidate to ask you questions about the position, ensuring that you:

- Outline the job description in greater detail, giving an overview of their potential role in the company.

- Discuss salary if not mentioned already; provide them with details on the pay and conditions associated with the position.
- Answer any remaining questions.
- Ask to check references and give a timetable for the decision and how they will be notified.
- Thank them.

Once a candidate leaves, allow time before seeing the next person in order to review their performance and prepare a written evaluation and weighted rating against the defined criteria. By doing so, you will have a set of completed evaluations at the end of the day and will be better able to identify the higher-scoring candidates, rather than trying to remember who was who. Also, take a break before the next interview so that you are fresh and ready to be as attentive as possible.

Of course, the majority of points covered here about interviews are fairly straightforward, and indeed most are well known, but despite this, research and my first-hand experience shows that they are not consistently applied by many managers. Your primary goal for interviews should be to find the best available candidate, so it's important that you approach this critical management activity from that perspective. However, if you consider the damage that even one bad hire can do to your business or department and how much time, effort and money you have to expend to clean up the mess afterwards – all of which are scarce resources these days – then that should also encourage you to pay more attention to ensure that you are not misled by unsuitable candidates.

A good place to start is to ask yourself how good you are, and have been, at keeping out bad apples.

Chalk and Cheese

"Put your tray on the belt when you are finished with it and slide it back through."

No response from the intended target of the shouting.

"SIR, put your tray on the belt when you are finished with it and slide it back through."

Still no response from the target. And even the shouter's colleagues looked somewhat bemused by his behaviour at this point, judging by the glances shot between them and the numbers of eyes thrown to heaven.

This is going to get interesting, I thought as I put back on my belt, shoes, watch and jacket before starting to pack my laptop into my carry-on bag.

"Are you DEAF, Sir?"

The intended target finally looks up.

"Are you talking to me?" he asked with all the menace that Travis Bickle used as he stared into the mirror in the movie *Taxi Driver.*

I didn't have time to stick around to see how it all ended as my own flight was being called and I had to dash to the gate, but I was totally with my fellow passenger on this one. It was very early in the morning, everyone was tired, and this security guy was just standing around barking orders at people; moments earlier, as I waited to go through screening, he had snapped at an elderly lady because she had forgotten about a little bottle of holy water in her handbag. Everyone in the queue watched as, in a hectoring tone, he lectured someone who was old enough to be his grandmother. He was clearly unhappy in his job and definitely in the wrong career.

In contrast, no more than half an hour later I was 10,000 metres or so up in the air and being asked in a pleasant friendly tone whether I wanted tea or coffee with my breakfast by a no-doubt equally exhausted but professional flight attendant. *Chalk and cheese.*

The two incidents got me thinking about how individual employee performance can fluctuate greatly. Although the two people in question were working for different organisations and were employed in very different roles, it was clear that they were not at the same level of performance. You will have had similar experiences in managing your own people, maybe not to the same degree of fluctuation, but some of your team members will outshin/ terms of both the way they do their jobs, and the results they achieve. attempting to get the most from all staff, which no doubt is a pressing priority for you just now, we often treat them as a homogenous unit when in fact they are individuals with varying levels of performance.

Most companies these days have fairly advanced systems and procedures for marketing to their customers and, as part of this, managers fully understand that segmenting their consumer base is essential because they know that there is no such thing as a 'typical' customer. Rather, there are different types that can be grouped or segmented according to their common needs, preferences, behaviours and in terms of what they deliver to the business (high and low value, etc.). This concept, amongst other things, allows owners and managers to better focus their marketing efforts and can also help to tailor products and services to each specific segment. Segmentation can also be applied to an organisation's employees.

1. Segmenting Employees

What I mean here is segmenting employees in a structured manner according to performance, and not just with the broad brush-strokes that you probably use at present, as in full- or part-time, length of service, good and bad, or other general criteria. I mean really applying segmentation in a formal way with the same objective you have for your customers, namely to better identify and then respond to their needs. I believe there is significant scope for all businesses to think more intensely about the different segments of employees and then tailor what is offered to them.

Before continuing, you may well be concerned that if you do start to segment your people more formally, you may risk being accused of favouritism. And, yes, if you make the wrong choices here then that is a possibility; however, segmenting employees does not mean treating some well and others badly; it means giving them what they want and need in terms of their employment experience, just as you do for your customers' experience. For example, when it comes to your customers, giving your top performing segments something extra doesn't mean you treat lower producing categories badly, does it?

In my experience, very few managers acknowledge that the concept of segmentation can apply equally as well to employees and, if done correctly, can make a valuable contribution to engagement levels and business performance. When you think of it, however, no matter how big or small your team is, there is no such thing as a 'standard' employee in terms of their performance, is there? They each have differing interests, values, behaviours and are motivated by different things and, as a consequence, the contribution they make to the organisation also varies, often considerably. For instance, if you have an employee who is relatively happy in their job, works reasonably well, does what is expected of them but no more, and has no real passion for the business, can they be motivated and engaged to the same extent as an 'in a hurry' go-getter who consistently walks that extra mile for you? Probably not. Should their overall employment experience on a daily basis be exactly the same? Hardly.

So, how might you set about segmenting employees in a way that adds value to your business? Well, first of all, as with customers, it is simply not possible for you to meet the precise and ongoing needs of each and every employee, so segmentation is really a form of compromise which allows you to capture the common needs and expectations of different groups of employees into a small number, say four or five, segments. And what might those segments be? There are no set rules here, and you probably mentally segment your employees by performance to some degree already, but just as you did when you categorised your customer base, you need to focus on some relevant criteria which allow you to create definable segments that:
- are distinct and recognisable from the wider group of employees;
- can be targeted individually;
- have longevity – of course, employees will come and go but the 'segment' must have permanence.

As an example of different approaches in this area, Towers Watson, a leading global professional services company with expertise in employee engagement, promotes the concept of 'Sustainable Engagement'. This describes the intensity of employees' connection to their organisation, based on three core elements:
- The extent of employees' discretionary effort committed to achieving work goals (being engaged)
- An environment that supports productivity in multiple ways (being enabled)
- A work experience that promotes well-being (feeling energised)

The key attributes fundamental to each element of sustainable engagement are:

Traditional Engagement	Enablement	Energy
• Belief in company goals and objectives • Emotional connection (pride, would recommend employer) • Willingness to give extra effort to support success	• Freedom from obstacles to success at work • Availability of resources to perform well • Ability to meet work challenges effectively	• Ability to maintain energy at work • Supportive social environment • Feelings of enthusiasm/ accomplishment at work

Based on a statistical analysis of their employee engagement surveys, Towers Watson categorise respondents into four distinct segments, as shown in **Figure 13.1:**

Figure 13.1 Towers Watson Employee Segments

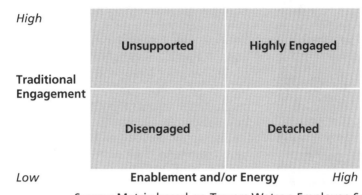

Source: Matrix based on Towers Watson Employee Segments

Further details of these segments include:

Highly engaged: Those who score high on all three aspects of sustainable engagement.

Unsupported: Those who are traditionally engaged, but lack enablement or energy for complete engagement.

Detached: Those who feel enabled and/or energised, but lack a sense of traditional engagement.

Disengaged: Those with less favourable scores on all three aspects of sustainable engagement.[31]

As a second example of a route to segmentation, BlessingWhite,[32] another international expert in this area, describes five employee segments that vary according to an individual's level of contribution to a company's success combined with his or her job satisfaction. These are shown in the table on page 70.

These are just two examples of how the segmentation of employees could be addressed in your organisation. You might adopt a different approach more suited to your needs – and, if you do, make it as simple as you like to start with. In terms of helping to identify segments (and indeed in defining where each employee fits) a useful tool for providing the necessary information can be an employee satisfaction or engagement survey, but how helpful that is for you will

---

[31] Towers Watson, "Engagement at Risk: Driving Strong Performance in a Volatile Global Environment" (Global Workforce Study 2012), p 5.
[32] BlessingWhite, *Beyond the Numbers: A Practical Approach For Individuals, Managers, and Executives*, Blessingwhite Employee Engagement Report 2011. See www.blessingwhite.com/EE2013

The Engaged	• *High contribution and high satisfaction* A most desirable group, yet one that still needs attention. Employers must keep these workers engaged or risk them falling into one of the next three segments.
Almost Engaged	• *Medium to high contribution and satisfaction* A valuable group within reach of full engagement.
Honeymooners and Hamsters	• *Medium to high satisfaction, but low contribution* Being relatively new to the company, 'Honeymooners' are happy to be there although they haven't yet figured out how best to contribute. Hamsters, however, may be working hard, spinning their wheels, yet contributing little to the success of the company.
Crash and Burners	• *Medium to high contribution, but low satisfaction* These workers perform well, but are disillusioned and dissatisfied with the company. They have the potential to become totally disengaged while negatively influencing other employees.
The Disengaged	• *Low to medium contribution and satisfaction* This group is "the most disconnected from organizational priorities, often feel underutilised, and are clearly not getting what they need from work". If these workers can't be coached to higher levels of engagement, an exit strategy would benefit both employee and the company.

Source: BlessingWhite

naturally depend upon what questions it includes and, if you already conduct such surveys, what information it currently provides you with. Another mechanism to facilitate segmentation can be the company's appraisal process and again if that is well thought through and rigorous, it can assist you in identifying even basic employee segments, such as a scale with top performers at one end of the spectrum and under-performers at the other.

It is also worth noting that, like any business, you will have the odd outright negative employee, but I personally would not formalise them as a 'segment' because, as mentioned above, a segment should have longevity and you certainly shouldn't tolerate negative employees over the longer term. Remember, a 'low performer' or a 'disengaged' employee is different from a consistently bad performer who is likely having a damaging impact.

Once you have defined segments of employees appropriate for your business, what then?

2. The Employee Value Proposition

With employee segments defined, you then want to get a handle on what works best for each of those segments in terms of the overall employment experience you provide, and this is where the Employee Value Proposition (EVP) comes in. EVP relates to the totality of the employment experience available at any given company. It is about much more than wages and benefits and includes culture, development opportunities, rewards, leadership, teamwork, and so on. In fact, EVP is concerned with everything that impacts on the experience an employee has whilst working for your business.

A good way to view EVP is to consider it as being the *deal you make with your people*: what you will offer them in return for their skills, knowledge, experience, dedication and hard work. Again, we are quite comfortable talking about value propositions in relation to customers, but applying that principle to employees doesn't always meet with the same degree of acceptance by employers. This can result from a fear that, as some managers have said to me, being seen to 'pander' to employees will lead them to believe that they hold all the cards in the relationship. Those concerns are perhaps understandable to a degree but it isn't about pandering and this is very much a two-way street; the EVP is what you offer your employees in return for what they give you. It's a trade-off, and it's a worthwhile one because your business benefits as a result of keeping your top performers for longer and having them more engaged and productive.

Focusing on a value proposition for employees is also recommended because it forces you to think in broader terms of creating worth for people across the entirety of their work experience, rather than just concentrating on individual components such as wages, benefits, perks, etc. The concept of EVP is not new, but at a time when budgets and resources are tight within most businesses it can be more challenging to plan for and develop.

How can you develop/improve your organisation's EVP?

First, let's look at some research about EVP. According to the Corporate Execeutive Board (CEB) in the US which has studied this area extensively,[33] "an effective EVP provides organizations with three quantifiable benefits:
- *Improved attractiveness*: Companies and organizations that have defined and meaningful EVPs can source employees from a much wider pool of talent. For example, the top performing companies, i.e. those with the most effective EVPs, can draw candidates from about 60% of the labour market, including

---

[33] CEB, *Attracting and Retaining Critical Talent Segments, Building a Competitive Employment Value Proposition,* Executive Summary, (2006, Arlington VA).

'passive' candidates who would otherwise be content to stay with their current job. Lesser-performing organizations are able to source only from the most active 40% of the labor market.

- *Greater employee commitment*: Organizations with effective EVPs enjoy significantly higher levels of commitment from their employees. In fact CEB indicates that in those organizations with really effective EVPs, 30–40% of their workforce display high levels of commitment, compared to less than 10% in under-performing organizations.
- *Compensation savings*: Organizations with effective EVPs can reduce the compensation premium required to attract new candidates. Top-performing organizations are able to spend 10% less on base pay compared to under-performing organizations."[34]

You don't need to be an expert in human resource management to understand that employees, particularly those in the top percentile, will migrate towards those companies offering the best proposition or overall package. In terms of formalising your company's EVP, or building on the one you have, there is no one-size-fits-all approach, but you can consider the attributes shown in the table on page 70 as you seek to create a compelling EVP.

Clearly you will already have some type of an EVP in place, every business does to some degree, although you may not call it that, or indeed have communicated it as effectively as you might. As you seek to better define your EVP, or to expand on what you already have, some steps to consider include:

Identify the Most Attractive EVP Elements Generally, and by Employee Segment

The first step in building or expanding your EVP is to be very clear as to what matters most to the type of people you are seeking to recruit and retain; you therefore need to define what elements of the EVP are most attractive for all employees generally and then for each of the particular segments you define. And just as you do with customers, use focus groups with members from each employee segment to determine what they feel would help to engage them more with the business.

Conduct an Assessment of your Current EVP

Once you have a clearer picture of what matters to your employees, it's a good idea to compare your current offering to see how it stacks up. As you do so, consider:
- what your organisation's current strengths are in terms of an EVP;
- whether you are currently meeting employee expectations with the EVP you offer, especially in relation to your competitors;
- how well you currently tailor your EVP to the variety of employees you have;
- which EVP components best reflect your strategic focus and business ethos; and
- what is practical and sustainable over the long term with regard to an EVP.

---

[34] *Ibid.*

How do you reward people and recognise performance?	How do people progress and advance?	How do you treat employees?	What type of work do you offer?	How do relationships function in the business?
– Pay and Conditions – Benefits Package – Holiday entitlements, etc. – Performance-related schemes – Recognition schemes – Perks and bonuses	– Career opportunities – Company growth/ expansion rates – Learning and Development opportunities – Promotion philosophy – Mentoring programmes	– Approach to engagement and empowerment of employees – Credentials as an employer of choice/awards won – Levels of diversity – Grievances and disciplinary procedures	– Job design – Interesting/ varied/ meaningful work – Location of business – Opportunities to travel – Work-life balance – Empowerment and autonomy – Delegation policy	– Management ethos – Management styles – Approach to teamwork – Communication channels – Social networking

Build the EVP and Communicate it Effectively

From your research and analysis on this issue, you will have garnered the information you need to develop your EVP in a manner which best matches the expectations of all employees in the organisation, and each segment, but that also aligns to your strategic vision for the business. Remember, even applying the EVP model, every employee is still treated fairly and in accordance with all employment legislation requirements, but you will tailor certain aspects of the experience such as training, rewards, delegation, etc. and other components of the EVP in order to best match the expectations of different employee segments.

It's then a matter of communicating that EVP and its component parts to prospective and existing employees. This may sound like an obvious step, but even in small companies employees are frequently unaware of some of the benefits potentially available to them; there is no point in having a compelling EVP if nobody knows about it. As part of that communications process it can be useful to develop a summary statement that captures the essence of your EVP, or better still build such sentiments into your existing mission statement. Of course, it goes without saying that you must subsequently deliver on the EVP you communicate; failure to do so will lead to lower engagement levels and ultimately higher turnover.

When you pay attention to the subject of recruiting and retaining employees, you will frequently see it described as a 'war for talent'. Finding and keeping the best people is extremely hard today, and getting harder, so if you want your organisation, department or team to outperform the norm then you cannot ignore the role your employees will play in achieving that goal. Consequently, you should not overlook the benefits that could arise if you define clear employee segments, then create and communicate a compelling and segment-tailored EVP which attracts the right people, enhances their engagement levels, raises productivity and reduces employee turnover.

And in doing so, bear in mind that what works for chalk won't necessarily have the same impact on cheese.

Gi ve More to Get More

"Imagine for a moment that your employees are balloons. And also imagine that each balloon has a weight hanging from it by a piece of string. When a balloon fills with helium, it naturally rises upwards. Think of the helium in this context as being the positive aspects of the people in your business – their knowledge, skills, motivation, commitment and overall performance: the more helium the better, right? The weight on the other hand represents the negative, the things that hold us back, drag us down, and prevent us from rising higher; some of this might be skills or knowledge gaps, or it could be down to personality-driven issues."

This was an analogy used by a facilitator on a programme I attended. It was a good mental image that has stayed with me, and I would expand it slightly to say that there are broadly three types of people in any business:
- Those full of helium, your top performers.
- Those with more helium than weight holding them down so they rise, however slightly (this is where most employees are).
- Those with more weight than helium.

While this is a somewhat tongue-in-cheek generalisation, in any business there will be people of varying motivation levels and abilities. It's your job as a manager to try to get the most from each of your employees, which in turn requires you to develop them, in various ways, and appropriate to their level of contribution to the business. In that sense, developing people is a significant part of your role and especially so at times like these when you are trying to maximise the contribution that each individual team member makes. While there are any number of activities that can be classified under 'development', the emphasis here will be on three important areas: training, coaching and mentoring.

What you do in relation to training, coaching and/or mentoring shouldn't be viewed in isolation, although that is often precisely what happens in a lot of companies. Broader issues such as the overall culture within your organisation and prevailing attitudes towards staff are important when it comes to getting the most from any development activity, so it's worth highlighting a few general points that impact on the potential for success of your efforts:
- 'Culture' is the collection of values, beliefs, norms and customs that make any company what it is – you could even say that culture is the *personality* of an organisation and differentiates it from similar entities. Culture impacts heavily on day-to-day business life, and, therefore on employee development. For example, if a wider people-oriented culture, in which employees feel valued and respected, is lacking in your business then any expenditure on training,

coaching and/or mentoring is pointless or at least diluted. You don't need a degree in psychology to understand just how irrelevant development becomes for employees who are badly managed on a daily basis, or who feel undervalued. If the wider culture in a business is essentially broken, then anything spent on developing people is potentially wasted.

- How decision-makers within the organisation view development is also important. When I sit and talk with senior managers about growing their businesses, they generally think in terms of return on investment: *What's the return on this particular investment going to be?* is how they think as a rule. Yet I always find it slightly amusing that when many of the same managers look at the development of their people, something suddenly changes, and the focus frequently turns to the cost side alone: *What's this going to cost me?* In my experience, if the investment mindset is applied to all development activities, it is surprising just how quickly outcomes improve when *What's this going to deliver for me?* serves as the mantra.

- Equally, we have all heard operational managers and supervisors use the excuse that they "don't have time" to develop their people. Again, with an investment focus, they will come to recognise that failing to train, coach and mentor their employees, amongst other things, makes them less efficient and ultimately less productive and, as a result, significant management time is lost fixing the problems that arise. By front-loading the time in terms of developing their staff, the return is improved quality and productivity, as well as time freed up for the more important management activities.

With these general points in mind, the following three sections offer guidance specifically in relation to getting the most from training, coaching and mentoring.

1. Gaining from Training

If you want to maximise the returns generated from any employee training you provide, you need to think about two important factors, *content* and *contribution*:

The Content of Training

While it may appear obvious to say that the content of training offered to employees must be tailored to their needs, while at the same time remaining focused on what is best for the business, this is still a common failing in how training is delivered in many organisations. For example, sending a group of employees on a generic customer care course, or a number of managers on a standard development programme is of questionable value to either the business or the people involved. Yet, this kind of thing happens all the time, mainly because it's easier to organise; employees are frequently lumped together and shunted off to training programmes which have little direct relevance to them, or to courses pitched at levels that are entirely inappropriate for their needs.

Sure, generic training in areas such as customer care is applicable to all employees but there is really no such thing as a 'standard' training programme, and this is even more applicable when it comes to personal development at a management level. A golden rule should therefore apply: training programmes should always be tailored by employee segment (see **Element 13**), and any employee or manager attending a course must clearly understand its objectives and how that particular event fits into their wider development plan. When they see its purpose, they naturally strive to learn as much as possible from it and are more likely to later apply that learning for the benefit of the business.

Linked to the content issue is the quality of delivery, whether the training is provided in-house or by external consultants. Again, it's fairly basic to say that the delivery of training must be stimulating and engaging if it's going to have a positive impact, but how many times have you seen employees trudge out of a training course at the end of a session, or day, looking as if they had been forced to dig coal for a few hours? Badly delivered training is a waste of time, no matter how good the content.

The Contribution of Training

A second point to consider when seeking to maximise the returns from training is the ability to measure its outcomes; quantifying the impact of training delivered not only supports cost–benefit analysis, but also helps to better target future expenditures. Unfortunately, when it comes to measuring training outcomes in concrete terms, the approaches managers use are frequently quite ad hoc. For example, in many companies the only real evaluation of training comes from the assessment sheets filled out by attendees at the end of a course; this is useful information in terms of validating content and delivery, but it doesn't give any insight at all into whether the training provided later translates into positive outcomes back at work. This perhaps goes some way to explaining why owners and managers are often so quick to cut the training budget when hard times hit; it's difficult to justify expenditure for an activity where the returns are all too frequently described in vague terms. Making the case to senior management that training leads to increased morale, improved quality, reduced staff turnover, etc. is hardly a winning argument from a hard-nosed business perspective, valid as those claims may be.

In his seminal book, *Evaluating Training Programs: The Four Levels*,[35] Don Kirkpatrick has defined a four-level evaluation model which covers:
Level 1: Reaction
To what degree participants react favourably to the training.
Level 2: Learning
To what degree participants acquire the intended knowledge, skills, attitudes, confidence and commitment based on their participation in a training event.
Level 3: Behaviour
To what degree participants apply what they learned during training when they are back on the job.

[35] Kirkpatrick, *Evaluating Training Programs: The Four Levels* (Berrett-Koehler 2006).

Level 4: Results
To what degree targeted outcomes occur as a result of the training event and subsequent reinforcement.[36]

This is a very useful model for addressing how to better evaluate the training you offer, and there is no pretence that doing so is easy. It is not. The key is to try to link the outcomes from all training activities to specific business measures such as customer satisfaction, employee satisfaction, sales, cost reductions and individual performance results.

2. The Power of Coaching

Of course, formal training is not the only route to developing your employees. Coaching and effective management also go hand-in-hand, in the sense that much of what you do is concerned with helping employees to raise their performance on a day-to-day basis. For this, you need to be a good coach, and in that regard there are two types of coaching to consider: *corrective coaching* and *performance coaching*.

Corrective coaching relates directly to situations where an employee is struggling with a particular task, or skill, in their job; the willingness and motivation are there but they are having some problems getting it right. They don't need formal training as such, but might require corrective coaching just to help them get that final piece of the puzzle into place. This is relatively easy to address because the focus is on task, and once you approach the coaching in the right way, there are rarely too many problems other than the employee who simply cannot master a particular skill to the level required.

Performance coaching, on the other hand, is broader in scope and seeks to resolve short-term or periodic attitudinal and behavioural issues that are affecting an individual's results. For that reason alone, the performance coaching of others is the greater challenge for any manager and will be the primary focus here.

Performance coaching can take place in a variety of scenarios, ranging from a directive approach by you to one of facilitation:

Problem identified by:	Manager	Manager	Employee	Employee
Solution identified by:	Manager	Employee	Manager	Employee

Directive —————————————————————➤ **Facilitative**

Depending upon the issue at hand, and indeed the employee involved, there may be times when you are forced to be directive in terms of how you coach others; on occasion they refuse to respond to your efforts, so you end up mapping out the problem for them and also determining the solution. Clearly, this has limitations, as the employee is not taking ownership of the situation. At the other end of the scale, you use your talents to facilitate the employee to both define the problem and the solution. This is a far preferable approach as the person involved

[36] Source: www.kirkpatrickpartners.com

is essentially directing their own development; that said, it takes a lot of skill for you to be able to draw out the problem and then guide the employee to find the solution. In between these two approaches are situations where the employee might raise a problem with you and you offer guidance on the solution, or where you raise the issue but lead them towards defining the best way forward.

Regardless of which performance coaching scenario is involved, you should keep the following points in mind:

- Simply telling a difficult or under-performing employee to change their attitude or behaviour is likely to have limited impact because in most instances they probably don't even think there is an issue in the first place – more likely, they believe it is you who has the problem.
- For that reason, the first goal of performance coaching is to get the employee to accept that there is a difficulty to be addressed and also that you are not willing to allow it to continue. As in the above scenarios, they might do so readily on their own but, more often than not, you will have to coach them towards that acceptance.
- When operating in coach mode, your ability to remain calm and in control is of course vital. Some troublesome employees may know exactly which buttons to press and, if you react, then not only will the coaching fail, but you will have given them the pleasure of winding you up.
- The ability to use all your communication skills to good effect – question technique, listening skills, managing tone and body language – lies at the heart of being an effective coach.
- When faced with a significant attitudinal or behavioural problem, be realistic about your goals in terms of outcomes. It is unlikely you will see a radical turnaround from one coaching session, but if you see progress in the right direction, then that is an achievement in itself. It usually takes a number of attempts to get to your ultimate goal.

Performance coaching is a really valuable skill for managers because every employee has at times attitudinal or behavioural issues that need to be addressed. Unfortunately, some managers regularly by-pass the coaching route altogether and, when faced with performance-related problems, even relatively minor issues, rush too quickly into disciplining people, even though coaching might have resolved the matter. In most cases, it's better to try coaching initially because once you head down the disciplinary route you change the dynamic of the relationship with that employee and it rarely fully recovers, in my experience. Clearly, if someone fails to respond to genuine coaching attempts, it may be necessary to then shift into disciplinary mode but that will always be the exception not the rule. Coaching, when done well, works.

Finally, on the issue of coaching, its use is primarily intended when dealing with periodic negativity or infrequent problem behaviour from a person in your team. When faced with an overtly negative employee who is serving as a continuous disruptive influence, it is unlikely to have any great impact so you need to consider how you deal with such individuals. **Element 15** will help you to do just that.

3. Making the most of Mentoring

The late Hugo Chavez considered Fidel Castro to be his. Richard Branson says that Freddie Laker was one for him. Apparently, Ayrton Senna played the role for Rubens Barrichello. And even Steven Spielberg considered Stanley Kubrick to be his. I am talking about mentors.

In all walks of life, mentoring is an important cog in the development wheel; although it is probably more accurate to say that mentoring can be an effective development tool, but only when mentoring programmes are well-designed and managed. It is important to understand that mentoring can produce negative outcomes if not managed effectively and there are many reasons why mentoring relationships can break down, from badly defined schemes to unrealistic expectations on behalf of either party. Still, for all the potential pitfalls, there are numerous findings which show that effective mentoring makes a positive contribution to both individual and business performance. One important study[37] highlighted both the benefits and potential drawbacks associated with formal mentoring programmes:

	Major Benefits	Potential Drawbacks
Organisation	• Development of managers in the organisation • Reduced turnover • Increased organisational commitment • Low costs or cost-effectiveness associated with formal mentoring programmes • Improved organisational communication.	• Lack of organisational support • Creation of a climate of favouritism • Difficulties in coordinating programmes with other organisational initiatives • Costs and resources associated with overseeing and administering the programmes.
Mentee	• Career advancement • Personal support • Learning and development opportunity • Increased confidence • Assistance and feedback.	• Neglect of core job • Negative experiences • Unrealistic expectations • Overdependence on relationship • Role conflict between boss and mentor.

[37] Douglas, *Formal Mentoring Programs in Organizations: An Annotated Bibliography* (Center for Creative Leadership 1997).

	Major Benefits	Potential Drawbacks
Mentor	• Personal fulfilment • Assistance on projects • Financial rewards • Increased self-confidence • Revitalised interest in work.	• Lack of time • Lack of perceived benefits • Lack of skills needed for mentoring role • Pressure to take on mentoring role • Resentment of mentees.

These, and many other benefits, have been highlighted time and time again in a range of reports over the years and, when well-managed, the potential downsides associated with mentoring programmes can be overcome, or at least minimised. Here are some general points to consider about effective mentoring programmes.

Mentoring Model

Any successful mentoring programme must consider four interdependent dimensions: the business, the programme, the participants and the development:

- *The Business* Programmes should be both people-centric and business-focused in approach so that they meet the needs of all those involved, yet fit within the strategic vision for the organisation.
  - Does the culture within your business currently support the mentoring concept?
  - Are there already strong relationships between your senior and more junior managers and/or key employees?
  - Are you willing to provide the necessary resources and support to underpin the mentoring programme?

- *The Programme* Programmes should be structured, but flexible enough to allow relationships to develop naturally over time.
  - What will the programme look like? Will it be confined to senior executives mentoring more junior managers, or will it also be targeted at including 'fast-track' employees? Could it also involve middle managers mentoring some employees?
  - What are the specific goals for such a programme in your business?
  - What will the mentoring programme entail? What development areas will it target?
  - How will mentors and mentees be matched up?
  - How long will the relationship last for each mentor-mentee grouping?

- *The Participants* Mentoring is relationship based, so issues such as trust, confidentiality, communication skills and compatibility are all important considerations and need to be accounted for when you design and implement the programme.
  - Will the mentors and mentees be committed to the concept?
  - Do the mentors have the required mentoring skills at present? Is training required to support them?

- *The Development* Programmes should have a broad development focus and the key areas for supporting mentees should be defined so that all mentor-mentee relationships focus on similar themes: management style, communication, business planning skills, etc.
  - How will the expected developmental outcomes for each individual be defined?
  - Can you use a management competence model to help define the broad development areas that could be addressed through mentoring?
  - How will individual development needs be dealt with under the mentoring programme?

By considering the above factors and thinking through questions such as these, you can devise an approach that has the right balance of formality and informality, which pairs the mentors–mentees for best effect and has defined common development areas so that all relationships focus on similar needs.

Mentoring in Action

To create a timeline for your mentoring programme, you could pair mentors and mentees for a period of one year. After that the pairings can be rotated; and by doing so every 12 months each mentee gets to interact with, and learn from, more than one manager – and particularly it might be necessary to pair certain mentees and mentors together in order to help an individual to develop specific skills on their development list. Of course, all mentors will approach the mentoring role in different ways, but there are certain phases that all mentoring programmes should follow:

- *Phase 1 – Initial Contact* The initial phase of developing the mentoring relationship should be seen as a 'getting-to-know-you' time, whereby the participants meet – as required – on an informal basis to develop a rapport between them, and to start building a bond of trust. The environment created at this point is obviously critical, as it will set the tone for the remainder of the relationship. It is also useful at this early stage to discuss how both parties view the mentoring relationship developing, and to clarify perceptions about what the process is likely to entail; the mentor should encourage the mentee to broadly identify how he or she sees their career progressing in the short- and medium-term future. This information will be useful during Phase 2 of the process. In effect, clear but informal 'terms of reference' should be agreed between each pairing and the logistics of the process finalised. This phase might happen during the first month.

- *Phase 2 – Identification of Development Needs* As highlighted, it's important that a broad field of development areas be devised for the programme, based on your management competence model (see **Element 23**), so that all mentoring relationships focus on similar things. Within that overall template, the priority needs of each mentee still need to be defined. Once the mentee's development areas have been identified, it is important that they are then prioritised and the most relevant gaps addressed in that coming year. It is critical too for the mentor not to be over-ambitious about how much he or she can be of assistance to any particular mentee – no one manager can have the skills and knowledge to help in all development areas. So, the mentee's needs must be matched as far as is possible with the capabilities of the mentor. This phase might happen during the second month.

- *Phase 3 – Development* Once the needs are identified and prioritised, and goals for the year ahead established, it is then a matter of determining how the mentor can support the mentee in these areas. It should be up to each mentor–mentee pair to collectively determine how often they need to meet to address the agreed development needs, but minimum contact requirements should be devised as part of the programme to avoid 'drift'. This phase goes on for the greater part of the year.

- *Phase 4 – Evaluation* It is important for the mentor and mentee to regularly review progress, both to address the development needs and review how the relationship is evolving. What's more, a broader evaluation of the programme is necessary and this can be attained through appraisals, by examining core metrics such as management turnover rate and indeed via individual performance measures for participating managers and employees. This overall evaluation should happen after each annual mentoring cycle.

The points covered here are intended to give a flavour of what is required to manage an effective mentoring programme and of course there are related concerns about ensuring that all mentors have the right attitude and skills to make the most of the initiative. Yes, it can be a challenge to set up and manage an internal mentoring programme, there's no denying that fact, but the key is to find the right level of formality and to devise an approach that suits your business and has commitment from all those involved.

Finally, developing your employees at various levels, particularly managers, is not optional these days because if you really want to get the best from people then you must continuously train, coach and mentor them so that they have the skills and attitudes to deliver at a high level. Clearly, maximising the returns from these activities is never easy, but it's worth the effort when you consider that doing so is good for employees, customers, you and ultimately for your business.

In short, the more you give in terms of employee development, the more you get in return.

Watch Out, There's a Bad Apple About

Early in my managerial career, in the late 1980s, I was faced with a very difficult employee who made my life a misery for well over a year. In a highly unionised workforce, beset by ingrained inflexibility coupled with a strong 'Them and Us' culture, he certainly knew how to play the game to his advantage. Any request was met with some form of objection or query. His work was done, usually late, and generally to a very poor standard. It would take him twice the length of time to complete a task as anyone else; and more times than not you would have to redo it, in part at least. He frequently arrived late for his shift and was out 'sick' on many occasions, with the added bonus that he was one of those aggressive, bullying characters who enjoyed a battle. He received several verbal and written warnings but for some reason he had the support of the shop steward who in turn was a very domineering character. Senior management opted for industrial peace at the expense of really dealing with problem issues, including this guy. I was told on numerous occasions, "don't let him get to you", or "just ignore him", which wasn't very encouraging when you knew that you didn't have the support of those further up the chain of command. Worse still, he knew that too.

And he was very clever; for all his problematic behaviour, and in all the years he had worked with the company, he had not quite ventured into the realm of gross misconduct and done something for which he could have been instantly dismissed. When he reached a second written warning, he would behave himself for six months or so whereby, according to the rules at the time, his slate was wiped clean again. My experience of dealing with him was comparable to being exposed to low doses of radiation on a daily basis. I still remember the frustration and annoyance I felt at that time.

Thankfully, the world of work has changed dramatically since then. As a result, truly difficult employees are rare these days but not so unusual that you won't have had to deal with at least one in your career, and that you will not be faced with others in future. Dealing with persistent problem behaviour is a real challenge, frequently raised with me by managers at all levels and in all fields. Often people who fall into this category get broadly categorised as 'bad apples'. In **Element 12**, the focus was primarily on how to keep them out of your business; here the emphasis will be on what to do when they have already slipped through the net.

At this point, it is important to note that there are two categories of negative behaviour that require different responses.

1. Temporary Difficult Behaviour

Things will happen in any organisation which might cause employees, individually or collectively, to turn sour for short periods. People have personal issues that can affect their performance, and there are a range of occurrences at work which can generate a degree of unhappiness among all employees. Perhaps a decision taken, a misunderstanding, or a problem faced will turn the mood nasty for a while. In reality, everyone has the potential to be 'difficult' on occasion, so dealing with employee-related problems of that nature is simply a fact of life and all managers have to regularly face such issues at work. Handling these temporary occurrences is relatively easy if you think about the following points:

- What trigger has caused the difficult behaviour you are seeing? Have you any control over that trigger? If yes, can you change things to alleviate the problem?
- If no, can you at least communicate with the individual or group on the matter? Sure, you may not be in a position to solve the underlying issue, but listening always helps.

As identified in **Element 14**, part of the solution here is to use your coaching skills and in most cases if you do the right things in that regard then you can move beyond the problem.

2. Ingrained or Prolonged Difficult Behaviour

This type of behaviour is somewhat different and occurs when certain individuals spend a large proportion of their working lives in a difficult state, often without any real reason. They struggle to be positive, cooperative, engaged and can display a whole host of other problem behaviours. Often, as in my opening example, they are fairly clever too, in that they are not so problematic as to warrant dismissal, but they manage to walk that fine line, often for some time. Though, as also mentioned, such characters are in the minority these days, you still need to worry about them because, apart from the obvious challenge they present to your authority, if allowed, they can do significant damage to the morale of others.

It is this ingrained behaviour that causes most stress for managers, I find, and when it does arise it's the type of thing that can keep you awake at night. In an important study on this issue, Will Felps, Senior Lecturer at the Australian School of Business, and his colleagues,[38] have defined three categories of difficult team member behaviour, which they argue is especially likely to 'spoil the barrel' if left unchecked:

1. *Withholding of effort* 'Withholders' intentionally dodge their responsibilities to the group and free ride off the efforts of others. Some examples of withholder behaviour include things like "not completing tasks or contributing adequate time, not taking on risks or responsibilities, or not disclosing

[38] Felps, Mitchell, and Byington, "How, When, and Why Bad Apples Spoil the Barrel: Negative Group Members and Dysfunctional Groups" (2006) *Research in Organizational Behavior*, pp. 181–230.

aptitudes in the hope that others will compensate." In everyday terms, Felps describes these characters as '*slackers*'.

2. *Being affectively negative* This, the researchers argue, typifies a person who continually expresses a negative mood or attitude. They also found that inherently negative individuals were more likely to "exhibit an awkward interpersonal style and to more frequently express pessimism, anxiety, insecurity, and irritation". In doing so, they affect the motivation and mood of others. These are alternatively described as '*downers*' according to Felps.

3. *Violating important interpersonal norms* The researchers described individuals in this category with the truly lovely phrase 'interpersonal deviants'. In addition, they identified seven common behaviours associated with such characters: making fun of someone, saying something hurtful, making an inappropriate ethnic or religious remark, cursing at someone, playing mean pranks, acting rudely, and publicly embarrassing someone. In plain speaking, Felps describes these individuals as 'jerks'.

These categories are more than someone having a bad day, or underperforming in the short term. Of particular interest in this study was what Felps and his colleagues highlighted about the impact that bad apples of one kind or another can have on group effectiveness and outcomes. They found that "having a bad apple in a group will have a negative impact on the group production-related processes of motivation, creativity, and learning as well as on the integrative processes of cooperation and conflict. Without these processes in place, groups fail." In other words, these characters are not merely annoying or frustrating for others in the group, but directly damage the team's overall performance. Additionally, Robert Sutton,[39] a professor at Stanford University and bestselling author of *The No Asshole Rule*, argued that bad apples are "remarkably contagious" and that leaders who ignore them are "setting the stage for even their most skilled people to fail".

You are certainly already familiar with the annoyance value of bad apples but the clear message from the research is that they can do a whole lot worse than annoy if you let them. This links to a final point worth pinpointing in Felps's research which relates to the common responses to bad apples in the workplace. Essentially, apart from avoidance, the researchers grouped the reactions as follows:

• *Motivational intervention* – this describes the range of actions undertaken to change negative behaviour through the application of influence tactics, which might include positive activities such as coaching, or negative responses such as the withholding of praise, respect, or resources until the behaviour changes.

• *Rejection* – actions intended to minimise or eliminate interaction with the negative member, which can either mean ejecting them from the group or, if that's not possible; isolating them – in other words, sending someone to 'Coventry'.

• *Defensiveness* – described by the research team as those acts which are intended to protect and repair one's own sense of autonomy, status, self-

---

[39] Sutton, *The No Asshole Rule: Building a Civilized Workplace and Surviving One That Isn't* (Reprint edition, Business Plus 2010).

esteem, or well-being. In other words, when people feel powerless to get rid of the problem individual, some begin to respond in negative ways themselves and this is one way in which bad apples – if not dealt with – bring the worst out in others. This is why avoiding the issue is particularly harmful.

It's therefore clear you cannot ignore prolonged dysfunctional behaviour, but the key question of course is what can you do about it? As you know, there's no magic answer to this, but here are some general considerations:

- Managers who have encountered such employees have often told me that they allowed the individual in question to "get under my skin" to the point where it almost became an obsession to get rid of them. That route, while understandable, is the very last thing you should do; easier said than done I know. The moment you allow emotions to drive your actions in these circumstances is the time you lose the ability to think rationally, so you need to avoid that at all costs.
- Focus on performance not personality. Often in these circumstances, the negative employee will try to shift discussions onto the personality side of things: "you just don't like me" or "you're picking on me", and so forth. This is simply a form of deflection and you always need to be very clear as to how they have deviated from the expected level of performance, with specific examples of what they have done wrong.
- It is also important at an early stage to notify your superior and indeed HR that there is an issue and that you are attempting to resolve it. Once it moves beyond run-of-the-mill problem behaviour it's time to flag it for others. You will still try to manage your way through it, but they now know it's an issue and can monitor progress from afar.
- Of course, you do need to begin by attempting to coach the individual through the difficulty. In doing so, you might want to read up on the coaching guide covered in **Element 14** and if you can achieve even small improvements then, in this context, that is an achievement in itself. Unfortunately, particularly difficult employees can be virtually impossible to coach, or to change in any meaningful way, but you do as a first step need to genuinely try and not just go through the motions.
- If they do not respond to the coaching, then it's often useful at this point to get another manager – your boss, or someone from HR – involved, to play a mediation role, whereby they try to bring a fresh perspective to the relationship and see if they can bring the employee around.
- If that doesn't work, then you are left with no alternative but to shift towards a more directive approach. Until this point, you should have avoided overtly threatening them with consequences, but now the employee needs to be made aware of what must change, what support is still available to him or her, but also what the potential outcomes from failing to improve will be. Then, rather than dealing with every minor daily issue that arises, you might review progress every two weeks, or monthly, and discuss what changes have been seen, or not as the case may be.
- Failure to respond to this more directive approach will unfortunately require you to move fully into a disciplinary process as set out in your organisation's standard procedures.

This may seem like a very drawn-out process, but unless the employee has done something entirely unacceptable, or completely against the rules, it's one you need to follow. Failure to do so will potentially result in you having to deal with an unfair dismissal claim. When I discuss this issue with managers, even the very experienced ones, I can often see the frustration in their eyes; undoubtedly, employment rules are at times weighted in the employee's favour, but there is little alternative than to work through a process similar to that above. It's also why ensuring that you keep such characters out of the business in the first place through effective recruitment is so vital.

Throughout the many years I have spent advising managers on this issue, part of the problem I frequently see is that, as mentioned, some allow the conflict to turn into a battle of wills with the individual in question; doing so will cause you untold stress, so you must avoid falling into that particular trap. Whatever you do in confronting bad apples, it's important to be proactive about it – especially these days as you cannot afford to carry even one negative employee – as well as being structured and consistent in your approach because, as Robert Sutton puts it, "the behaviour of assholes damages individual well-being and also impacts corporate profits, mostly because it reduces people's commitment to the organization and drives out some of the best employees."[40]

Have you any bad apples spoiling the barrel at present?

[40] McLaughlin, "Interview with Robert Sutton on *The No Asshole Rule* for the Workplace," *Management Consulting News*, 2012.
www.managementconsultingnews.com/interviews/sutton_interview.php

Boxing Clever

During the London Olympics, I heard Gerry Hussey, psychologist for the Irish boxing team and one of the leading sports performance psychologists in Europe, interviewed on radio. He made some compelling points about managing the performance of the boxers, which I believe are applicable to the world of work and worth sharing.

Hussey began by explaining that while talent is of course vital for success, the attitude each boxer brings to the ring is equally as important. Nothing new there, perhaps. He then went on to highlight that it's how that positive attitude is moulded and applied over time that really matters. For example, when the coaches work with the boxers they never focus on medals, but rather concentrate solely on performance, which makes sense when you think about it because medals only begin to matter if the performance is at the level required; thinking about 'winning' too early could actually be a distraction. The coaches avoid focusing on medals because, in the first instance, having selected the boxers for the elite programme, they already know what each individual is capable of (what '100%' looks like for every one of them) and they understand that if they can get each team member to perform as close as possible to his or her maximum capability in every fight then, come medal time, they will be in the running.

Even more interesting perhaps is how the coaches and boxers collectively manage performance during a fight itself. Rather than seeing a bout as comprising three rounds of three minutes each (for men), they break it down into 30-second sections – so a fight is actually made up of 18 segments during which a range of strategies is deployed, and they are always focusing on one 30-second interval, or "controllable section" at a time. A fighter might be out-boxed in one of those sections, or indeed may win that segment, but in either case the focus quickly shifts to the next one. This is an interesting way of managing performance: focusing on milestones and not solely on outcomes, balancing short- and longer-term considerations.

The final area that Hussey discussed during the interview was how the boxers are managed away from the ring. He pointed out that on the day he was interviewed, since the start of the Olympics the team had already spent 10,080 minutes (one week) in the team village, but most of the fighters had only been in the ring for 27 of those minutes. Managing the downtime was therefore just as important as managing the intense lead up to, and duration of, a fight.

So, what relevance does this have to your daily experience at work?

First, the obvious link: an employee's attitude is just as important to his or her performance in business life as it is in the sporting arena. But the issue of translating overall goals into controllable sections is an interesting one in terms of how performance can be better managed at work. Often in business life we seek to drive employee performance based on desired outcomes or goals, without focusing enough on the milestones needed to deliver the required end result. There is certainly scope to do more in a work context in terms of managing immediate, intermediate and long-term performance. Equally, just as the coaches manage the boxers away from the ring, how managers deal with performance during the natural peaks and troughs that occur between the busy and quieter periods in any business is something that isn't always given the attention it deserves. However, when you really think about it – and particularly if you operate in a customer-driven environment – keeping your people fresh and ready for those intense periods of activity is just as important in business life as it is in boxing.

In terms of raising employee performance, let's explore some more advice from Gerry Hussey. In a presentation he gave back in 2008,[41] he made the following observation about how he and the coaching team had transformed their approach to lifting boxers' performance. "We overlooked the importance of consultation and partnership. We had many 'experts' yet we forgot to consult the most important expert…*the athlete.*" He explained the basic but crucial point that their efforts to improve the overall success rate of the Irish boxing team had actually begun with listening to the boxers – they brought them to the table and really tuned into their thoughts and concerns. He further explained how they had essentially done three things as a result. They had:

- stopped handing the athletes ready-made solutions;
- encouraged the boxers to come to them with questions and concerns; and
- made them effective, proactive and responsible decision-makers.

He further emphasised that "decision is the key to transformation. It is one of the primary character traits distinguishing high performers." And the outcome of this shift away from a top-down, 'here's-what-you-do' approach? According to Hussey "the team discovered a huge wealth of untapped knowledge among our athletes and developed an increased atmosphere of self-belief and self-respect." He added: "the boxers very quickly began to develop their own language of performance and in doing so they began to discover that the answers were within their own grasp and understanding. We discovered that the most important voice in athlete development is the voice of the athlete."[42]

These principles apply just as well in the work arena, and when we talk about employee engagement it is precisely this type of transformation that we are seeking to achieve. If you want to drive performance in your business, you first have to truly listen to, and involve, your people. Through that partnership process they will engage more fully with you and the business – or at least the majority

---

[41] Hussey, "From Obedience to Responsibility", Presentation by Gerry Hussey to the National Coaching Forum DCU, 13 September 2008. See www.coachingireland.com/files/gerry-hussey.pdf
[42] *Ibid.*

will do so. Gerry Hussey summarised the experience with the Irish boxers this new partnership system we believed that we were now developing rou...ne decision-makers as opposed to routine followers." Sadly, on occasion, I have seen the opposite happening in some organisations.

Considering the lessons gained from the Irish boxing team, what other practical things can you do to raise the performance of the people in your company? Well, plenty really, but without engaged employees most of those efforts would be wasted, so do not underestimate the importance of generating and sustaining buy-in among team members for what you are trying to achieve. It goes without saying that to really bring out the best in your people they must clearly understand what is expected of them; more importantly, perhaps, they need to recognise how their daily efforts contribute to achieving your company's business objectives.

1. Meaningful and Immediate Goals

Every employee in your business should have clearly defined goals, relevant to their level and position. While all staff are likely to already have job descriptions, which are essential, such documents focus on what you want them to do, not necessarily what you want them to achieve. So, alongside job descriptions, you need to individualise your goal-setting process so that everyone in the business is aiming at something tangible, and that something should be linked to your overall business goals. And yes, you can also have shared, or team goals, where appropriate.

As part of setting goals for employees, you should also think about how you can break down those goals into more measurable sub-goals, or milestones, just like the 30-second segment concept applied to the boxers' fights. Establishing a formal goal-setting process that focuses not only on the end result, but also on intermediate and ongoing performance – and which does so for each employee – is therefore vital. Monitoring and measuring individual performance against those milestones and goals will ultimately deliver better outcomes for your business.

2. Where's My Medal?

Of course, it's not possible to talk about the issue of raising employee performance without highlighting the rewards that they expect in return for that extra effort when it is delivered. In the amateur boxing world, you might argue that they have medals to spur them on, and that's undoubtedly a driving force, but if you also consider that approximately 300 boxers competed in the London Olympics with only in the region of 50 medals up for grabs then the motivated-by-medals argument is not the only answer.

That said, in a work context, there is rarely the same level of intrinsic desire to succeed as seen in boxers – at least not for all employees – so it's no secret that the key to retaining the best and brightest talent and getting the most from them lies in both recognising and rewarding top performance. *Recognition* can take many forms and need not be financial; in addition to that, it is also necessary to think about appropriate *rewards*, such as a pay-for-performance model, if you do not have one already. This may well pose some logistical challenges, and how rewards are structured (described below) is a vital consideration; however, it's worth the attention you give this area because such a system allows you to track individual employee progress against performance goals, identify who is delivering on expectations and who is not, and, ultimately, to raise productivity and motivation by recognising and rewarding exceptional effort.

The manner in which you reward people, if not structured properly, can have unintended consequences, which are worth reflecting upon at this point. For example, in the early 1990s, Sears Auto Centers[43] in the US decided to pay commissions to mechanics based on the number of specific repairs they performed in a given month. It was an all-or-nothing deal, either the mechanics hit a certain number and they received the bonus, or they didn't and got zilch. By the end of each month nearly every customer who brought a car to Sears was told by their mechanic that they needed a repair, e.g. new brakes. Since most customers trust their mechanics, they mostly agreed to the work. The mechanics reached their targets and received their bonuses. Sears made millions of dollars from unnecessary repairs. They later lost it all in fines, and damaged goodwill, when the truth was discovered. Badly structured reward systems can promote negative behaviour.

When thinking about your current approach to recognition and rewards, consider the following questions:

Do you have a Good Mix of Financial and Non-Financial Incentives?

Having a variety of rewards is important and, although money talks, there's plenty of evidence around to show that the impact of non-financial rewards is not insignificant. One such example is highlighted in an article by McKinsey & Company[44] which showed that "three non-cash motivators: praise from immediate managers, leadership attention (for example, one-on-one conversations), and a chance to lead projects or task forces are no less or even more effective motivators than the three highest-rated financial incentives: cash bonuses, increased base pay, and stock or stock options."

The message is not to underestimate the importance of non-financial rewards. Indeed, many similar studies have shown that, for people who are happy with their existing salary level (and that's key here), some non-financial rewards are more effective than extra cash in building long-term employee engagement, and this applies across sectors and job roles, particularly so in the current economic climate where additional earnings are likely to be highly-taxed in any case.

---

[43] Gellene, "Sears Expected to Settle Auto Repair Charges", *Los Angeles Times* 2 September 1992.
[44] Dewhurst, Guthridge and Mohr, "Motivating People: Getting Beyond Money" (2010) 1 *McKinsey Quarterly*, pp. 12–15.

Are your Reward Systems Fair?

This sounds like such an obvious requirement that it hardly warrants mention, but there is also evidence to show that employee attitudes are positively influenced by reward systems that are not only fair, but more importantly are seen to be so. In my experience, and particularly in smaller companies, reward systems can often be ill-defined or lacking in structure and worse still they are frequently applied inconsistently, which means that the whole system can create suspicion and distrust amongst employees. You need to be sure that all your reward mechanisms are transparent and objective in their application, and just as important, are seen to be fair by one-and-all.

Are you Rewarding the Right Things?

As well as being individual- and business-focused, are your reward incentives reflective of your core values and beliefs? Do they promote the type of positive behaviours that you want to see in your people? Of course, most companies reward employees for increasing sales, reducing costs, etc. and such reward schemes are vital as they drive business results. On the downside, as the Sears example above shows, badly designed rewards can promote negative behaviours so you want to make sure you don't fall into that trap. However, there may well be other opportunities for recognition and rewards which are in line with what you stand for as a company that can promote good behaviours as a result. For example, if you are making real efforts to be environmentally friendly or corporately responsible as a business, do you have incentives to encourage the behaviours you want to see in this regard?

Are your Reward Mechanisms Encouraging Short-Term and Long-Term Focus?

It's not an exaggeration to say that many organisations, particularly financial institutions, became obsessed with the short term over the past decade and this thinking naturally affected their reward mechanisms. It's important to find balance here. You need to see improved performance from your employees today, not at some imaginary point in the future, and therefore you will want to reward your people in the short term. But in doing so, you need to be very sure that as they chase those rewards they are not doing damage to the long-term prospects for your business; as would be the case, for instance, if your salespeople were mis-selling or applying pushy sales tactics just to meet targets, or if your production team were cutting corners and putting quality at risk in order to keep costs down.

These are just some points to consider about your reward mechanisms and it's worth taking a step back to see if what you do at present is contributing to raising the performance of the many and not just the few, and whether it's helping the business to grow in a sustainable way. Simply put, rewards are good, if they promote positive behaviour that improves short- and long-term business performance. The following **Element** offers more interesting views on the limitations of rewards and incentives.

The final point to take away here in terms of managing employee performance is the important role of the coach. Undoubtedly the role of a sports coach differs in many respects from your job as a manager – and particularly with regard to the fact that such coaches usually only deal with highly motivated and talented individuals. That said, how they interact with and support the athletes under their wing, and how they help them to push for greater effort, offers guidance in what you must do in terms of lifting the performance of your team. A big part of what any modern manager must do is to coach his or her employees and that looks likely to become an even more important activity for you in the coming years.

Are you helping your people to box clever at present?

Re wards Re-Think

Imagine someone asks you to assist them with a simple experiment. You agree to it, and they bring you to a quiet room where you see the following items lying on a table: matches, a box of tacks and a candle.

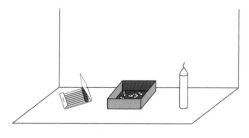

The researcher then explains to you that, using only the items on the table, the aim of the exercise is for you to find a way to fix the lit candle to the wall in such a way as to ensure that the candle wax doesn't drip onto the table below. They then leave you alone for a while. How would you go about it? No, really, think about it for a moment before reading on. What solution might you propose?

Most people who are faced with this conundrum think of a few common possibilities: some consider using the tacks to fix the candle to the wall. Others propose lighting a match in order to melt the side of the candle and then stick it to the wall; apparently, none of those solutions work, or at least not very well. The true solution is to empty the box of thumbtacks, put the candle into the box, use the thumbtacks to nail the box (with the candle in it) to the wall, and light the candle with a match as shown. Sometimes, we fail to see the box as having any other function than to hold the tacks but it can be used to solve the puzzle.

Now, 'The Candle Problem', as it is known, was first presented by Karl Duncker, a behavioural psychologist, as far back as 1945, but it has become a popular example used widely these days – although not solely for problem-solving purposes as you might think – but as a useful way of highlighting some important issues about motivation. For example, in his recent bestselling book *Drive: The Surprising Truth About What Motivates Us*,[45] author Daniel Pink uses the problem to explain how much of what we think about incentives in business life is actually wide of the mark. He reminds

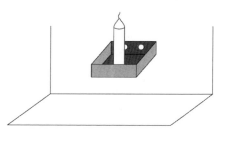

[45] Pink, *Drive: The Surprising Truth about What Motivates Us* (Riverhead Books 2011).

us of a study in the 1960s which was conducted by Sam Glucksberg, a well-known Professor of Psychology at Princeton University, who used the task to explore the power of incentives.[46] Glucksberg gathered his participants in the study together and then separated them into two groups, giving them the following instructions:

- He told one group that he was going to time them individually to determine how long it typically took people to solve this type of problem.
- He told the second group that they would get a reward for completing the task. He further explained that if they were in the top 25% that solved the problem fastest they would get $5.00. He also added that the person who was the fastest of all would get $20.00. (The rewards sound small today, but back in the '60s when he conducted this exercise, they represented a good incentive for what was likely to require only a few minutes' work.)

How do you imagine things turned out? The incentivised group, if our views on rewards are correct, should outperform the non-incentivised one, right? Wrong. On average, it actually took the second group, the incentivised bunch, three and a half minutes *longer* to solve the problem than it took the first group. In other words, the people without external incentives completed the task much faster than those who were incentivised. This pretty much goes against the common thinking about how we drive performance. As a form of control, Glucksberg later repeated the same experiment, except this time, when he presented participants with the box, it was empty and the thumbtacks were on the table beside it. (In other words, he made the problem easier because once the box wasn't being used as a container it took less mental agility to be able to assign a different function to it.) This time, the group that was being rewarded finished the task a lot faster than the other group.

Pink uses Glucksberg's findings to emphasise that the accepted premise in management circles is that incentives produce better results, not worse, but this experiment (and many more like it, by the way) consistently show that the *get this for doing that* approach to incentivising people may well work in some circumstances, but it actually has negative consequences in many situations. He further explains how he has spent many years studying motivation and has found a strong mismatch between "what science knows and what business does" on the issue of motivating people; he believes that the approach to motivation in business life is centred around a carrot-and-stick model which may work in some scenarios but less and less today where creativity is required. He further emphasises that the *get this for doing that* reward model tends to succeed for tasks that are well defined, where the rules are clear, where the destination is obvious, but when a bit of creative thinking is required then they don't work, and in fact can do more harm than good.

Now, when he first promoted this view, even though all the research verified what he was saying, Pink was met with a barrage of scepticism. Having anticipated it, he was armed with some solid evidence to back up his argument. One such example refers to work done by another Dan – Dan Ariely – a leading

[46] Glucksberg, "The Influence of Strength of Drive on Functional Fixedness and Perceptual Recognition" (1962) 63 *Journal of Experimental Psychology*, pp. 36–41. In the public domain.

economist and top-selling selling author of books such as *Predictably Irrational*.[47] Ariely and his colleagues at Massachusetts Institute of Technology (MIT) conducted a study with students[48] in which they gave them a series of games and offered three levels of reward for their performance at each game: small, medium and large rewards. The better they did on a game, the larger the reward they received.

When a game involved only mechanical skill the bonuses worked as expected and raised performance. But once the task required the students to think about the outcome and/or to be creative, the rewards actually led to worse performance. And just to ensure that there was no cultural bias at play in the study, Ariely took the experiment to India where the results were the same.

Actually, the more you think about these findings in practical terms the less surprising they become. If, for example, I work in telesales, where for every successful sale I make I get a reward and more sales equals more rewards, it's easy to see how a financial incentive might make me strive to achieve more; the process is broadly the same for each call. I'm not saying there's no skill involved, but there's not a whole lot of thinking or innovation required. But, if I were charged with coming up with a new product, or a better way of doing something, a financial reward might actually serve as a distraction; the ability to be creative, or to find solutions doesn't just happen at the flick of a switch – time is required – and if I worry that it's taking too long for the light-bulb moment to arrive, or if I am afraid of missing out on the reward, then that will naturally disrupt the creative process.

So, if financial rewards and incentives have only limited application, how can you get the best out of your people in today's workplace? Through his research, Daniel Pink, along with many others, has found that 'intrinsic' motivation is increasingly important: in other words motivation that comes from inside an individual rather than from any external or outside rewards such as financial incentives. Social scientists are increasingly finding that motivation stems from having a real desire to do something, or because we enjoy doing it, or when we feel that we are part of something bigger. Daniel Pink summarises this new thinking around three areas:
- Autonomy – the urge to direct our own lives
- Mastery – the desire to get better and better at what we do
- Purpose – the desire to be of service to something bigger than ourselves.[49]

If you stop for a moment and reflect upon this issue it starts to make a lot more sense. These three areas really do matter to people in daily work life. And in my experience, interacting with managers and employees across countries and

---

[47] Ariely, *Predictably Irrational: The Hidden Forces That Shape Our Decisions* (Revised edition, Harper Perennial 2010).
[48] Ariely, *et al.*, "Large Stakes and Big Mistakes" (2009) 76 *Review of Economic Studies*, pp. 451–469. doi:10.1111/;1467-937X.2009.00534.X.
[49] Pink, "The Puzzle of Motivation", *Ted Talks*, July 2009. See http://www.ted.com/talks/dan_pink_on_motivation.html

cultures, people at all levels want to fill their day doing something of value, and to feel that they are more than a number, or there simply to implement the decisions of others. Sure, money matters, and in fact the more routine and repetitive the job is, the more the focus probably needs to be on financial incentives. But, and think personally here, no amount of money would compensate you if you hated what you did every day, would it? Genuinely, some of the most frustrated and disgruntled people I have encountered in organisations were those who were highest paid. Other aspects of their role, like being micro-managed or working for a boss who undervalued them, meant they were still unhappy. So 'reward' is about a total package of measures (financial and non-financial) and the important message to take from this Element is that you should rethink what you currently do in this area in order to make sure that whatever mix you offer works best for your business and produces the highest return on investment.

Not Just the Score

"…and what did you score yourself for Communication?"

"Let me see…oh yeah, I gave myself a four for that."

"No, no, I don't think you're at that level just yet, I gave you a two point five."

"But I …"

"And how did you rate yourself for Teamwork?"

"Actually, I gave myself a five for that, as I always try to help my colleagues in ev…"

"A five? No, no, again that's a bit ambitious I think. Five means perfect. Nobody's perfect. I gave you three point five for that."

"But, but, I always…"

"And what did you score yourself for Customer Focus ... bearing in mind what I just said?"

"Well, I had that at five too, but you'll probably say it's a three or something …"

And on and on the 'appraisal' went, the employee in question later explained to me. She also said that she had become increasingly disillusioned with the review as the session advanced to the point that, by the end, she had more or less tuned out. The focus was purely on scoring each heading and getting through the session as quickly as possible, with little feedback or discussion taking place on her actual performance; and certainly no guidance given as to how to improve in future. In essence, she was told how she had performed and the improvements expected for the next period. Not an experience she was overly interested in repeating.

1. Why Appraisals Fail

Sadly, this is not an unusual outcome of appraisals in my experience. Now, don't get me wrong, not all performance reviews go astray for the same reason as above, but they do go astray, in that they don't deliver on the main goal to recognise employee achievements and to help them sustain and improve performance in the future for their benefit and that of the business. There are a number of studies that confirm that appraisals are not delivering what they might. One such example, a poll undertaken of 2,677 people (1,800 employees, 645 HR managers, and 232 CEOs) in the US, indicated that 98% of respondents found annual performance reviews unnecessary.[50] In the UK, a study of over 1,000 employees[51] highlighted that:

[50] Jozwiak, "Is It Time to Give up on Performance Appraisals?", *HR Magazine*, 22 October 2012.

[51] Badenoch and Clark, "Workplace Appraisals: Valuable Tool or Pointless Exercise?" http://insight.badenochandclark.com/general-news/28/11/2012/workplace-appraisals/8492/

- Over a third of UK workers believe appraisals are a waste of time and do not contribute towards their personal career development at all.
- Almost 55% of men and 63% of women admitted that they are not completely honest when evaluating themselves and others.

There are widespread concerns about the impact of performance appraisals in many organisations and, if the various reasons why appraisals fail, or under-deliver, were summarised, the list would include:

How They are Viewed

- Often you hear them described as 'appraisal interviews' when in fact they should be seen as 'appraisal discussions'. This is not a simple change in terminology, or playing with words; interviews largely symbolise one person extracting information from another, whereas discussions are two-way exchanges of information, which is supposed to be what appraisals are.
- Many managers, and indeed employees, see appraisals as one of those annoying tasks they need to get out of the way once or twice a year – a box to be ticked. They place little value on them, partially because they see few results arising from such reviews; in other words, nothing substantial changes for either the manager or the employee, so each year they put less and less effort into the process.
- Often, appraisal outcomes are tied to 'salary reviews' which is absurd if you think about it. Do you really believe that any employee will be honest about his or her performance (particularly weaknesses) if they know that the outcome of that meeting will influence whether they get a pay rise or not? My advice is always to keep appraisals and salary reviews separate; for example, hold the appraisal in mid-year, and the salary review at the end of the year. Then, depending on the level of improvement seen from the appraisal to the salary review, this will determine the decision taken on pay increases.

How They are Managed

- In many cases, and hardly surprising given the above points, both managers and employees under-prepare for the appraisal discussion so they are naturally ineffective. They are set up to fail.
- Sometimes the system takes over too and the focus is on scoring each appraisal heading, managing the paperwork around the process or completing unwieldy online surveys and the like. The system should always be a secondary concern.
- Often, appraisals fail simply because the manager involved lacks the skill necessary to effectively facilitate such intensive and potentially stressful communication events.

2. Appraisals Can Make a Difference

Despite all the potential pitfalls, appraisals – when managed effectively that is – provide a great opportunity for a structured review of an individual's progress, performance and results; in that sense, they are a critical part of your efforts to drive business improvement and, for instance, there's no point in talking about having a company-wide approach to goal setting and performance management if there isn't an effective appraisal process to support it. In addition, what is often overlooked about appraisals is that they are supposed to form part of your wider employee engagement efforts and unless they leave each employee feeling better about themselves as a result (even if they have had to recognise their shortcomings) then they have failed. And, yes, managing appraisals does require significant time and effort, but it's worth that investment because getting your performance reviews right can bring many benefits.

Benefits for the Business

Effective Appraisals can:
- Help to create an atmosphere of openness and trust within the organisation;
- Assist in developing closer working relationships between managers and employees;
- Highlight training and development needs (individually and collectively) as well as helping to identify organisational blockages which might otherwise go unnoticed; and
- Recognise achievement, and as a result, help to increase motivation which in turn can lead to greater productivity.

Benefits for Managers

Effective Appraisals can:
- Help to develop teamwork by removing the 'Them and Us' barriers between managers and employees;
- Provide managers with an opportunity to really listen to their people and to learn from those encounters;
- Help to give direction to each employee and by extension to the team as a whole;
- Contribute to generating respect between managers and employees; and
- Highlight work-related problems in specific areas/departments.

Benefits for Your Employees

Effective Appraisals can:
- Enable employees to receive considered feedback on their performance in a structured setting;
- Allow them to discuss their future with their manager so that they can see a career path for themselves;
- Assist with problem-solving, in the sense that an employee can raise any concerns they might have which helps their manager to address and solve those issues; and
- Identify their contribution to the company, leading to the preparation of a development plan for them.

To realise the above benefits clearly takes time and effort, but managers who treat appraisals seriously generally see a lot of rewards as a result.

3. Getting the Most from your Appraisals

To help you increase your effectiveness as an appraiser, you first need to prepare for the appraisal and this is usually where the process starts to go astray as frazzled managers rush the preparation phase. Of course, what needs to be readied will depend upon the precise performance management system in place in your company, whether it's an online model or manual system. Ultimately both you and the employee must review his or her performance against the defined criteria so that when you both turn up for the session you have something of value to discuss; yet, you both still need to be prepared to review the performance in an open-minded way.

When it comes to hosting the appraisal discussion, naturally you need it to be structured, and this can be guided by whatever appraisal headings you use. The principal aim of the review is to allow discussion to take place on an employee's performance in a relaxed environment. You will no doubt have your own opinion of their performance, and they will have theirs, but the objective is to get agreement on how they can improve with your assistance and support. Critical things to avoid include:

- *Focusing too much on scoring*: Discuss their performance against each of the relevant criteria in detail and afterwards agree a score for each item. The score or rating is really a secondary concern, what matters most is identifying strengths and areas for improvement.
- *Telling the employee how they have done*: It's much better to let them tell you first how they feel they have performed in a given area; at least that way you know whether he or she has a realistic assessment of their own performance (in comparison to yours that is) before you commit yourself.
- *Arguing over their performance*: If you find that you are arguing with an individual about every aspect of his or her evaluation, then clearly there are bigger issues at play which need to be resolved before a meaningful appraisal can take place.
- *Adopting a squirrel approach*: This means that you save up all your negative feedback for an employee and give them a lengthy dressing down at the annual appraisal. That's going to achieve little because an employee is not likely to take too kindly to receiving negative feedback about issues that may have happened months previously. Feedback should be ongoing for employees, and if you have had an issue with a particular individual, you don't return to it at the appraisal but rather focus on how things have improved, or not as the case may be, since the issue was last raised with them.
- *Ignoring the positives*: It's vital that an appraisal cover both the good and the bad, and too much of an emphasis on problem areas will only demotivate the individual.
- *Making it just about them*: Remember, a true appraisal allows the employee to raise issues with you that may be of concern to them, and that might even include aspects of your management style. In your past appraisals have you asked employees their views on how they see you as their boss? If not, why not? What were/are you afraid of? Not allowing them to do so undermines the appraisal process and most employees see that for what it is.

- *Dwelling on the Past*: In reviewing the past, it's important not to focus on it too much. The appraisal should look to the future and involve agreeing individual performance goals, targets and milestones appropriate to the role. In addition, it is necessary to identify their development needs and define how those gaps will be addressed in the next period.

All appraisals differ depending upon the nature of the employee involved, their length of service and so on, but when it is over both parties should leave feeling upbeat, with an agreed scoring of performance, a plan for the future that you both signed and an improved relationship as a result. How often does that happen at present? Of course, the required administration tasks need to be completed afterwards, but the really critical point in following up on an appraisal is that something concrete happens as a result, i.e. both parties must live up to commitments.

Finally, consider a last point here. During the appraisal process you too are under review by your employees and if you lack commitment to it or do not fully prepare yourself then they will notice. Yes, it's understandable that given the severe time pressures you are probably under these days, you might, intentionally or otherwise, devote less attention to appraisals than merited. But if you do so, your people will read a lot from that which in turn will come back to haunt you somewhere along the line. You will have scored a significant own goal if you allow that to happen.

And that particular score will matter.

Never Take Your Eye Off the Ball

If you have developed a high performing team you deserve a lot of credit, because it's never an easy thing to deliver. At the same time, it's important not to be complacent either because even the best teams can fail if ignored.

When a great team does go bad, it's often known as the 'Nut Island Effect'.[52] Nut Island was a sewage treatment plant located near Boston. For over 30 years, the plant operated effectively, so much so that senior management in the City's Water Authority paid little attention to it. After all, the team out there on the island was clearly a strong and effective one and they had proven time and time again that they could undertake their not-so-glamorous work in a diligent and safe manner, often finding innovative solutions to problems that arose. In essence they were considered to be a dream team. Then, out of the blue, the plant caused the worst environmental disaster in Boston's history, releasing billions of gallons of raw sewage into the harbour. How could things have gone so disastrously wrong? How could a team that had performed at such a high level, for so long, suddenly fail to that extent?

Paul F. Levy, a former Massachusetts state official, examined what had happened at the plant and in an article in the *Harvard Business Review* he first coined the term, 'The Nut Island Effect', which describes "a destructive organisational dynamic that pits a homogeneous, deeply committed team against its disengaged senior managers." What essentially happened at the plant – and this is a very quick summary – was as follows. The team out on Nut Island had proved over time that it could do the job required to a high standard. This in turn led to senior management having great confidence in the team, allowing them a high degree of autonomy and essentially leaving them to their own devices. They were considered to be self-managing. All good stuff, you may think; after all, it's never a good idea to micro-manage high performing individuals or teams. No it isn't, but complacency isn't smart either and that's essentially what happened here over a period of time. When the team at the plant asked for assistance, or requested additional resources from their senior managers, they were largely ignored because of the belief by management that the team at the plant could sort out whatever problems might arise, and why give extra resources to something that was already working well?

Over time, this lack of attention from senior levels caused widespread resentment amongst the team at the plant, they felt ignored and isolated and an

---

[52] Levy, "The Nut Island Effect: When Good Teams Go Wrong" (2001) March, *Harvard Business Review,* pp. 51–59.

us-against-the-world mentality set in. Funnily enough, this probably strengthened the bond between the team members but essentially meant that they closed off communication with their superiors; instead, they more or less devised their own way of running the plant, dealt with problems internally as they saw fit and ultimately began to hide potential difficulties from their superiors. Senior management, believing the team to be on track and on top of things, weren't in any way concerned at the lack of interaction; in fact their focus was elsewhere and they assumed that all was rosy at the plant when it wasn't. Eventually, the massive disaster happened, catching everyone off guard.

As Levy said "a team can easily lose sight of the big picture when it narrowly focuses on a demanding task. The task itself becomes the big picture, crowding other considerations out of the frame."[53] In this case, you could argue that the 'task' for the team at the plant became sustaining the *us-against-the-world* credo; they would show everybody they could do the job without any external support. Problems were buried and eventually it all came crashing down for everyone concerned.

Now, that's a very quick snapshot of an extreme example of what can go wrong when high performing teams are taken for granted. Depending upon where you work, it's unlikely that the same potential for disastrous consequences exists – for starters, your team, or at least the majority of them, are not likely to be located off-site from you. That said, the first lesson from the Nut Island experience for all managers should be that, no matter how well your team is performing, it is vital never to become complacent – even if the potential consequences of failure for your employees may not be as messy as they were in the case of Nut Island. A second, broader lesson arises too which is that your people always need your attention and focus, although the nature and level of that support must naturally change as the team develops.

You may at some point have come across Tuckman's stages of team development – "forming, storming, norming and performing" – as one model to describe how teams develop, or not. Briefly, the model suggests that, all going well, teams develop in fairly predictable stages from 'forming' (establishment phase) to 'storming' (when disagreements and personality clashes emerge) onto 'norming' (where things settle down and rules and norms are defined) and ideally to 'performing' (where the team is operating at full effectiveness). Whilst this is perhaps a useful framework for a project team, where all members come together at the one time and stay in place for the duration, it is not wholly appropriate in the workplace where teams are constantly changing as individuals join and leave. Instead, another option is for you to look at team development in a different way and rather than view it from a progressive model perspective, it is perhaps more useful to consider fluctuating 'states of team effectiveness'. After all, a team is judged on its ability to achieve the required outcomes, not necessarily on how long it has been in existence. Three states of team effectiveness can be defined as:

[53] *Ibid.*

Ineffective State

Teams can at times be described as ineffective from the point of view of achieving outcomes. There are many reasons why this might arise. It may simply be due to the fact that many of the members are new, so it is taking the team as a whole some time to get up to speed. Alternatively, it could result from the fact that there has been a breakdown within the team of some kind, perhaps if high levels of conflict have emerged, or maybe the problem is with you, or a decision you have taken that your people resent. Equally, a new work practice might have been introduced and the team could be considered ineffective on that particular activity until they master the new approach. In reality, there are many reasons why a team is ineffective and no team can excel on all occasions.

Excelling State

At the opposite end of the scale, a team might be deemed excelling when it is working well as a unit and outcomes are being achieved which consistently surpass expectations. At times, all teams can go through a purple patch where everything just runs to perfection and of course the goal is to build up a team which excels most of the time.

Effective State

In the middle, a team can be described as effective, which means it is generally working well and delivering on expectations. This is where most teams spend the greater proportion of their time.

These three states are perhaps a more accurate portrayal of what happens in the real world, and rather than progress through definable stages, your employees as a team can, and do, actually shift back and forth through these three states of effectiveness. Viewing teams as having the capacity to fluctuate between different states of effectiveness can be very useful as it offers you some guidance as to what management style to apply at different stages, because you obviously need to treat an excelling team differently from an ineffective one. For example, an ineffective team will need lots of direction and control from you, whereas a high performing team will need less of it (but never no direction and control). It is important to understand that being continuously attentive to your team is not the same thing as hand-holding or micro-managing. It is also worth spending a moment now reflecting upon your own employees:

- What state(s) of effectiveness do they operate in as a unit most of the time? Are there significant fluctuations? What is causing this?
- How does your management style vary in response to a shift in the state of effectiveness?
- What could you do differently to keep your team in an effective state more of the time, or better still to progress it to an excelling state?
- How does the climate in your team change with the state of effectiveness?

These are worthy considerations and you should think hard about how well you adjust your management style to match your team's needs at present.

The incident at Nut Island was undoubtedly an extreme case of what can happen when managers under-invest in their teams, but in less dramatic ways you can see Nut Island Effects happening in many businesses where groups of employees feel ignored or undervalued, or when their manager has one narrow style or approach that is deployed regardless of the team's state of effectiveness. You should always pay attention to your team and use your management style both to drive performance, i.e. to help them reach an excelling state, but also to respond when they have slipped back down the effectiveness scale for some reason. Failing to do so might not lead to such disastrous consequences as happened in Boston harbour, but that doesn't mean taking your eye off the ball couldn't result in some unpleasant outcomes and anything that reduces the effectiveness of your team is a bad result in the current climate.

Delegating Work Works, Provided the One Delegating Works, Too

"Say, Tom, let me whitewash a little."

Tom considered, was about to consent; but he altered his mind:

"No – no – I reckon it wouldn't hardly do, Ben. You see, Aunt Polly's awful partic-ular about this fence; it's got to be done very careful; I reckon there ain't one boy in a thousand, maybe two thousand, that can do it the way it's got to be done."

"No – is that so? Oh come, now – lemme just try. Only just a little – I'd let you, if you was me, Tom."

"Ben, I'd like to, honest injun; but Aunt Polly – well Jim wanted to do it, but she wouldn't let him; Sid wanted to do it, and she wouldn't let Sid. Now don't you see how I'm fixed? If you was to tackle this fence and anything was to happen to it – "

"O, shucks, I'll be just as careful. Now lemme try. Say – I'll give you the core of my apple."

"Well, here – No, Ben, now don't. I'm afeard – "

"I'll give you all of it!"

Tom gave up the brush with reluctance in his face but alacrity in his heart.[54]

That brilliant scene from Mark Twain's *The Adventures of Tom Sawyer* might seem out of place in a book on management, but it makes for a nice introduction to the topic of delegation. I am not saying that Tom offers us appropriate lessons on how to delegate – conning others into accepting a task is not to be recom-mended in a work context – but he does highlight the point that when some-thing is of interest to another person, it becomes easier to get them to take it on.

If I had a penny for every time I heard managers, and not only those at senior level, tell me that they "wished they could delegate more" I would be a very rich man indeed. And, apart from my own direct evidence, lack of, or poor delega-tion is a widespread concern in business life and is certainly a well-documented phenomenon. For example, a study of over 300 companies conducted by the Institute for Corporate Productivity[55] found that the majority of those polled

[54] Twain, *The Adventures of Tom Sawyer* (Dover Publications 1998).
[55] "The Time Management Practitioner Consensus Survey", Institute for Corporate Productivity (i4cp.com 2007).

indicated that they had serious concerns about time management and tion. The survey also highlighted that 53% had a "somewhat high" or a high level of concern about the time-management skills of their managers, and 46% of companies were worried about their executives' capacity for delegation.

There is a number of reasons why a manager won't delegate, or does so poorly, ranging from a propensity towards retaining high levels of control over all aspects of the workload, or a fear of what could go wrong if important tasks were given away, to a simple lack of understanding of how to delegate effectively. Research shows that the 'self-enhancement effect'[56] can come into play here too, whereby some managers have a tendency to judge the end-quality of a work task or activity more favourably when they have been directly involved in its completion; in other words, it's the old "nobody can do it better than me" fallacy and because delegation dilutes their involvement, some managers believe that the quality of outcomes will suffer as a result. Whatever the causes, in the busy environment that is the modern workplace, and with your 'to-do' list likely growing daily as you're expected to deliver more with less, if you do not delegate effectively this will cause you untold problems and ultimately it is you who will suffer as a result.

1. Factors of Delegation

In seeking to improve your delegation skills any analysis must first be considered in the wider context of employee empowerment. Although we often consider delegation within the limited confines of time management and/or management productivity, that's a bit too narrowly focused. Sure, delegation is undoubtedly important in that regard but it has much broader implications in the arena of empowering employees and this doesn't always get the attention it deserves. Delegation can be an important practical tool – for the right employees that is – in helping you to empower them. In that respect, four factors have been identified[57] as being important in relation to employee empowerment in general and I am adapting them here to relate specifically to delegation. They are: meaningfulness, competence, choice, and impact.

- *Meaningfulness* When deciding what to delegate, and indeed whom to delegate to, you should remember that it is vital for the employee in question to see value in the task or activity being delegated. In blunt terms, they have to care about it to the extent that it energises and motivates them to some degree. Tom managed to inveigle his friend into whitewashing the fence through a bit of reverse psychology, but any task you delegate has to have real meaning.
- *Competence* This relates to whether the employee has the skills to perform the delegated task and feels capable of successfully completing it. If you delegate, but do not support them, you will do more harm than good – they will likely fail, or at least under-perform which has implications for their self-esteem and

[56] Pfeffer *et al.,* "Faith in Supervision and the Self-Enhancement Bias: Two Psychological Reasons Why Managers Don't Empower Workers" (1998) 20, *Basic and Applied Social Psychology.* (Taylor & Francis Ltd; www.tandfonline.com. Reprinted by permission of the publisher.)

[57] Thomas and Velthouse, "Cognition Elements of Empowerment: An 'Interpretive' Model of Intrinsic Task Motivation" (1990) 15 *Academy of Management Review*, pp. 666–681.

this in turn will lead to them having a lower opinion of you because they will believe – rightly or wrongly – that you actually set them up to fail.

- *Choice* As will be highlighted shortly, if the employee has no choice as to whether to do the task or not, then that's not actually delegation we are talking about. Delegation only applies when you ask someone to undertake a task that is not currently part of their remit – it is part of yours.
- *Impact* This point links to meaningfulness in the sense that the employee should feel that accomplishing the delegated task will make a difference in some way, be that in terms of their own personal goals, for the broader benefit of the team or the organisation as a whole.

These factors are perhaps obvious but they are important when planning to delegate, and are frequently overlooked.

2. How to Delegate for Best Effect?

Ultimately, this is the key question for any manager. And in seeking to respond, it's important to recognise that what delegation actually entails is not always fully understood; the term 'delegation' is often used to describe a range of activities that involve getting things done in a work context. As a manager, you are accountable for others and there will be many duties and tasks that you will *allocate* to them in the normal course of the day. If these tasks fall within the remit of the employee in question then this is just part of your role as manager. This links back to the choice point made above: if the employee has to do it, then it's not delegation, it is allocation. The main concern in terms of how you allocate work is that you do so fairly, communicate your expectations effectively and ensure the employee has the necessary skills, knowledge and motivation to do the work in a manner that reaches your expectations. Most of what you do in terms of managing workload is actually allocation not delegation.

At the other end of the scale are tasks that you should do – they are part of your remit – but you hate doing them, like Tom's feelings about whitewashing, so you might fall into the trap of offloading them onto others. This is *abdication* and is not good practice, for obvious reasons.

Delegation lies somewhere in the middle. It involves passing an important task, which you are ultimately accountable for, to someone else. They don't have to take it on board, but do so for a variety of reasons which may include that they are ambitious and want to learn, or that they are simply just talented and helpful. Of course, the only value from delegating arises if you use the time you free up from having to do that task to focus on something more important; you manage your time better and become more effective as a result, or as Robert Half (founder of Robert Half International) said: "Delegating work works, provided the one delegating works, too…".

In seeking to become a better delegator, consider the following points:
- *Analyse your job* – what are the tasks that you could delegate to others and, if you did so, how could you use the time saved more efficiently? Consider the meaningfulness of those tasks.

- *Select the right person* – not all employees want to be delegated to so you need to define the right person and ask them if they would like to take on the task. You cannot force them to do it, as it falls under your remit. By the way, pulling rank on someone or using your position to subtly intimidate an employee into accepting to take on what is in reality part of your workload is never a smart move in the long term and will usually come back to bite you.
- *Delegation is a process* – you need to recognise that when you first delegate the task, you are likely to lose time not gain it. This is due to the fact that if it is an important and meaningful activity then you will have to spend time with the individual to train and coach them. As part of that, you need to communicate how to do it, explain the outcomes required and support them initially as they get to grips with it.
- *Delegate authority relevant to the job* – if the task requires your employee to request support and assistance from others, it is important that you communicate to all concerned that you have delegated responsibility to them for this task; otherwise, he or she may be faced with difficulties when requesting that support.
- *Monitor and review but don't micro-manage* – as you remain accountable for the task, you will always follow up to make sure it has been completed to standard, but once you are confident that your employee is competent at it, don't stand over his or her shoulder constantly – this means you haven't actually delegated the task and will likely lead to them feeling frustrated or believing that you don't trust them. It goes without saying that you should offer praise for a job well done.

Thinking about delegation in as broad a context as possible, viewing it as a process and really considering the many important aspects associated with it, will help to make you better at delegating. Mastering the art of delegation is potentially a win-win activity: when you delegate for best effect, you make yourself more productive, those you delegate to will develop a broader range of skills and, as a result, are likely to be more satisfied in their work and better prepared to move up in the organisation when an opportunity arises.

About
business

Consider important aspects of managing your business

All I'm doing These Days is Treading Water

"We believe a healthy society requires healthy and responsible companies that effectively pursue long-term goals. Yet in recent years, boards, managers, shareholders with varying agendas, and regulators, all, to one degree or another, have allowed short-term considerations to overwhelm the desirable long-term growth and sustainable profit objectives of the corporation."[58]

These are the opening lines in a call-for-action produced by the Aspen Institute, a respected international educational and policy studies organisation with a mission to foster leadership based on enduring values. Backers of the call included luminaries like Warren Buffett, James D. Wolfensohn and Bill George, plus a host of other leading international business, academic and political figures. This represents one of the many voices now railing against the folly of short-termism.

Every business owner or manager understands the need to step back and look at the bigger picture on a regular basis, to think strategically. In fact, few would disagree that looking to the future is vital. No, there is no argument on that front; a critical role for any senior manager is not to get caught up solely with the nitty-gritty of the here and now but rather to focus too on what's potentially out there on the horizon. Sadly, that's not how the reality of business life works for many managers. In fact, here's a flavour of some of the challenges I have heard expressed in recent times:

- Looking out onto the horizon becomes difficult when you have over 200 emails bombarding your inbox every day, many of which are pointless, but all need to be read, or at least scanned through.
- Looking out onto the horizon becomes difficult when cutbacks in management numbers over recent times now means that you spend much of your day doing work that others used to do.
- Looking out onto the horizon becomes difficult when your day is continuously hijacked by one meeting after another, so much so that you often only get down to your own work just as everyone else is heading home.
- Looking out onto the horizon becomes difficult when you have to face the board every four weeks and justify last month's numbers.

These are just some of the real and practical challenges that I have discussed with various managers as they rightly bemoaned the fact that, whilst they are

---

[58] "Overcoming Short-termism: A Call for a More Responsible Approach to Investment and Business Management" (2009) The Aspen Institute.

supposedly paid to think and act 'strategically', much of their focus has to be on short-term performance. Lack of future focus, whatever the cause, is damaging for business performance and it is not an exaggeration to say that many managers are frequently prevented from doing the very thing they are hired to do.

And, unfortunately, I don't have any easy answers on this issue, other than to stress again the importance of regularly making time to take a step back, even if you have to disappear up a mountain to do so. It simply has to be done. What is possible, though, is to offer you some questions to ponder when you do actually get time to think about where your business is headed. So, here are some important questions to help you reflect upon strategic concerns in relation to your business. And they are presented at three levels: your business, the competitive environment and the macro-environment.

1. Think About Your Business

Financial

- How has your business performed financially over the past three years? How did that compare to expectations? Have the year-on-year trends in sales and profitability shown positive growth, however small? How does your recent financial performance compare to other similar businesses and industry norms? Do you actually know? Are you leading or lagging in terms of key financial indicators?
- Are you truly optimising your revenues? Do your people up- and cross-sell for best effect? How effective are your pricing strategies? Are you over-competing on price?
- How well do you control costs? Do your managers have the knowledge and skills (and information) to really get a grip on expenses within the business?
- What's your predominant cash position? Are you doing everything you can to bring forward your cash inflows and delay your outflows for as long as is (legally and ethically) possible?

Customers

- Who are your customers? Have you divided them into relevant key segments? What are their specific needs by segment? Are you meeting, and more importantly exceeding, those needs? How have you tailored what you offer to meet differing consumer needs? Are you doing enough in this regard?
- Are you investing your time, money and other resources in a way that reflects the value of each customer segment, or are you spending too much on servicing unproductive customer groups?
- What do your customers think about you at present? Again how do you know? Is your feedback system broad enough so that you hear from a sufficient proportion of customers across all key segments? Do you regularly obtain both quantitative and qualitative feedback?
- When customers do give you feedback, how often do words like 'excellent' or 'outstanding' feature? How do your satisfaction ratings compare to industry norms and best-in-class companies? How do you measure loyalty at present?
- If you went out of business, why would your customers miss you?

Product/Service
- How does your product/service offering compare with that of your competitors? Where are the current gaps in what you offer? Why do they exist? Can you bridge those gaps, or should you change tack?
- Where do your products lie in terms of life-cycle? How are you preparing for the future in that respect? What new or enhanced products and services do you have coming down the pipeline that will give you an edge? What is unique about what you offer? How effective is your innovation process in terms of continuously enhancing your offering?
- How do your customers view you with regard to the products and services you offer? Are you considered by them to be a leader or a follower in your industry?

People
- How effective is your management team? What model or framework do you use to gauge their individual and collective impact?
- Are your employees fully engaged with the business? How do you know? Do you actually measure engagement levels? How does that result compare with the external benchmark? Have you segmented your employee base, defined a general employee value proposition, and then tailored it by segment? How attractive is your employee value proposition to prospective and existing employees?
- Do your people play an active or passive role in day-to-day decision-making? In what ways are they practically involved and empowered? Could you do more in this area?
- What's your employee turnover like at present? How does that compare with industry norms? What are you doing to keep your best people? Would you be considered an employer of choice?

2. Think About the Competitive Environment

Competitors
- How well do you know your competitors? Who are they? Where are they located? Do you have a lot of competitors, or only a few? Do they fear you or you them?
- What practical steps do you take to benchmark your performance against theirs?
- Why do your customers choose you over them, and vice-versa?
- In short, is your business considered a leader amongst your competitive set? Why?

Markets
- Are you operating in a mass market, or do you offer a specialist or niche experience?
- Is overall demand growing, or subsiding in your region?
- What drives the market(s) that you are in? Price, quality or both? What trends are you seeing in your markets? Are you increasing market share or losing it in your key markets?

- How does the market operate? Do customers buy directly, online or through intermediaries, or all three? Who are these intermediaries and what relationships do you have with them?
- How is technology affecting market dynamics?

Industry
- What are the key trends in your industry that will impact on your business in the medium term and beyond?
- What are the overall projections for the industry in the medium term?
- What supports are available for businesses such as yours? Are you maximising your usage of those supports? Who are the main business associations? Do you have a relationship with them?

3. Think About the Macro Environment

Economic
- What is the general economic outlook like for the short and medium term where you are? What is it like in the places where your customers come from?

Social
- How are consumer habits and needs changing generally? What implications might such patterns have for your business in the future?

Regulatory
- Are there any regulations on the horizon that might have implications for the operation of your business? What do you need to do to get ready for any such legislation/regulations?

Technology
- Are you maximising the use of information technology in your organisation, not only to deliver the best service possible for your customers, but to optimise productivity and efficiency, and to create internal learning platforms?
- What are the future technological developments that will impact on organisations generally in your field? How might they affect your business?

Environmental
- What are the key environmental issues that you need to respond to?
- How well do you manage your energy and waste removal costs? Are you proactive or reactive in this regard?

I don't pretend that any or all of the above questions are new, but they can serve as an important foundation in terms of helping you, and your team, to think more strategically about your business, once you have made the time to do so. An important point to mention here too is that, as you consider the future across these various dimensions, it is vital to ask yourself whether you are meeting your ethical obligations to all relevant stakeholders. Ethics should always be a strategic concern.

Rich Horwath, a highly-respected author and strategist, conducted research among senior managers from 154 companies, after which he defined four types of strategic thinkers. He later expanded on this in his book *Deep Dive.*[59] Here's what he came up with:

> Using the analogy of underwater diving, there are four types of strategic thinkers. The first group are the *Beach Bums*. Like a beach bum, this manager mentally lounges around and doesn't really contribute any insights to the business. The second type of strategic thinker is the *Snorkeler*. This type of manager skims the surface of issues. They're the first one to wave their hand in the air and say, "We have a problem" but don't offer any potential solutions. The third type of strategic thinker is the *Scuba Diver*. Like a scuba diver, when these managers are equipped with the right tools and instruction, they can come up with strategic insights. The final type of strategic thinker is the *Free Diver*. A free diver can dive underwater to depths of 800 feet on a single breath. These managers generate new and impactful ideas for the business on a regular basis.[60]

According to Horwath's research, only three out of every 10 managers are highly strategic, or at the Free Diver level. Which one best describes you at present?

I'll conclude with a comment from one senior manager I spoke to recently which links to this water theme. When discussing the issue of future focus, he said to me, "all I'm doing these days is treading water." And that unfortunately is a common challenge that all managers face, particularly right now: how to balance the demands of today, with the need to plan for tomorrow. **Element 22** now provides insights into the strategic planning process itself.

---

[59] Horwath, *Deep Dive: The Proven Method for Building Strategy, Focusing Your Resources, and Taking Smart Action* (Greenleaf Book Group Press 2009).
[60] Horwath, "The Three Disciplines of Strategic Thinking", available at www.strategyskills.com

Un der-exposure

You would imagine that if your company had grown exponentially since its foundation in the 1930s, you could expect to be around for a long time to come. You might presume too that when your brand name had become synonymous with an in-demand global product that the future would always be bright for you. If you had an overall market share of 20% in your field and a workforce comprising over 20,000 worldwide, that would also suggest the outlook is pretty bright, right?

That's no doubt what the senior executives at Polaroid thought at one point or other, possibly right up to the stage when the company filed for bankruptcy in 2001. Sure, there were many reasons for the demise of this once great brand, but a large factor was that the senior people in the company failed to adjust to new market realities. In essence, they stuck stubbornly to the belief that customers would always want hard-copy prints of photos. It turns out they didn't, or certainly not in anything like the quantities they once did. And by the time the executives at Polaroid realised the problem and tried to respond, it was too late; their whole business model was founded on the hard-copy concept and the revenues that came from film sales.

That might be a simplification of what happened, and the company – or at least the brand – has re-emerged, but this highlights the point that strategy matters, for all businesses large and small, new and old, high and low tech. In their book *Billion Dollar Lessons,*[61] authors Paul Carroll and Chunka Mui examined 2,500 failures suffered by publicly traded companies in the United States and found that the number one cause of failure was misguided strategy – not sloppy execution, poor leadership, or bad luck. So, strategy needs all the attention you can give it. A failure to have a clear strategy in the first place will kill your business, but so too will an inability to evolve and keep pace.

Unfortunately, what passes for strategic management in many companies, particularly in small and medium enterprises, is often more of the 'hit-and-hope' approach whereby decisions about the future are taken without adequate research or analysis and consequently are dependent for success as much on luck as anything else. Worse still, strategy formulation can at times stem from a 'follow the leader' mentality, whereby competitors simply copy what others do. It is not an exaggeration to say that in general there is room for improvement in how many companies tackle strategic management and firms which fail to master this critical

---

[61] Carroll and Mui, *Billion Dollar Lessons: What You Can Learn from the Most Inexcusable Business Failures of the Last 25 Years* (Revised edition, Portfolio Trade 2009).

function, if they haven't already, will pay the consequences as the business environment continues to pose significant challenges. In the previous Element, the concern was with making time for strategic thinking and some key questions to consider when doing so were identified. The focus here will be on the strategic management process itself – and it does need to be a structured activity – but in working through it, the process will be described in a way that's free from all the jargon that can at times accompany strategic management discussions.

1. Vision, Mission and Values

Would you do business with a company that made the following commitments to you?

> "Our mission is to build unrivalled partnerships with and value for our clients, through the knowledge, creativity, and dedication of our people, leading to superior results for our shareholders."

They sound like a pretty decent bunch to deal with don't they? If those words are to be believed, that is.

How about this business? Would you work with, or buy from, them based on the following?

> "Respect. We treat others as we would like to be treated ourselves. We do not tolerate abusive or disrespectful treatment. Ruthlessness, callousness and arrogance don't belong here.
>
> Integrity. We work with customers and prospects openly, honestly and sincerely. When we say we will do something, we will do it; when we say we cannot or will not do something, then we won't do it.
>
> Communication. We have an obligation to communicate. Here we take the time to talk with one another ... and to listen. We believe that information is meant to move and that information moves people.
>
> Excellence. We are satisfied with nothing less than the very best in everything we do. We will continue to raise the bar for everyone. The great fun here will be for all of us to discover just how good we can really be."

Sign me up now, you might think, given such compelling words. Sadly, if you were working with, or for, either of the above companies the reality would likely have been very different from their paper promises: the first example was a direct lift from Lehman Brothers' mission statement, and the second set of fanciful commitments was taken from Enron's values statement. As you well know, turns out that both those companies weren't exactly models of excellence, but rather are now bywords for how not to do things.

You lay the foundation for effective strategic planning in your business when you develop vision, mission and values statements, and they can make a real difference in terms of setting the overall context for your planning efforts. Unfortunately, most companies misuse such statements to some extent at least, with the result that the strategic planning process is generally flawed from the very outset; in other words, it's built on dodgy foundations. I don't mean that all businesses go completely against their public commitments to the extent that the Lehmans and Enrons of this world did in the end, but many businesses fail to get any real benefit out of having vision, mission and values statements. In fact, often the only reason they are prepared at all is because "everybody has them these days" as one business owner once said to me, or there's a gap in the front section of the annual report which needs filling in.

As a result of such sentiments, all too frequently, flowery but meaningless vision, mission and values statements are developed more as public relations tools than what they should be: true drivers of business success. A big part of the problem here is that many senior managers seem to believe that these statements are somehow the end-product of a process, when in reality they are only the beginning of one, i.e. strategic planning and management. So, a good first step is to truly understand what these statements are designed to do, because there is often confusion about the role of each. In essence, these statements, in broad terms, help you to start answering the question *Where do we want to be?* in relation to your business:

Vision

Your vision statement is concerned with the longer term future. In brief terms, it answers questions about your business such as:
- What are we trying to achieve?
- What do we want the business to become?
- What is the collective ambition driving us as a management team and group of employees?

Mission

If your vision relates to the desired destination, then your mission statement is all about the journey itself. Again, in broad terms, it describes how your business will operate in relation to your key stakeholders: owners, customers, employees, the wider community, etc. It sets out to briefly capture the answers to questions like:
- What will we deliver for our owners/investors?
- What are our customers' expectations and in turn what will we deliver for them? What will it be about our customer experience that will be unique, that they won't get anywhere else?
- What do our employees mean to us? What will it be about working for us that stands out from all the places our employees could work?
- What commitments are we making to the wider community?

Values

Values describe what really matters to those of you working in the business as you seek to live your mission and achieve your vision. These stated values in many ways help to bring your distinctive culture into life by expressing what concerns you.

So, what should you keep in mind when you set out to develop or revise these statements for your business?

- *Reflection is what really matters* The initial benefit in developing these three statements comes from the process of reflection and analysis that goes into preparing them. It's the act of stepping back to define what you are about and where you are headed that begins to add lasting value.

- *Consult widely* When developing, or indeed revising, your statements you should make the process as consultative and participative as possible; and if your business is to have real stakeholder focus, you and your management team should consult with your stakeholders to better understand what their expectations are. It is the outcome of these discussions which should help to inform what is eventually written down in the statements.

  In particular, when developing your values statement, your employees can play an important role in helping to contribute to the values that are agreed for the business. In fact, they might be encouraged to suggest values that are important to them for inclusion in the final statement, which will give them a sense of involvement as well as a degree of ownership. It is always vital to remember that, when individuals feel some attachment to the commitments made on their behalf, they are more likely to strive to live by them.

- *There are no rules* In setting out to develop (or revise) the vision, mission and values statements for your business, be as creative as possible and if broad statements aren't your thing then just use memorable phrases, or a motto which has meaning for you. If three statements sound too unwieldy, just have one, once it incorporates the right principles. If terms like 'vision', 'mission' and 'values' sound too formal, then call them something else. Always challenge your business to reach new heights but be realistic too, as unrealistic statements add little value in the long run.

2. Developing Strategic Goals

When you have prepared or revised the statements, what next? As mentioned, devising your statements is only the first small step and the true benefit in having vision, mission and values for your business will only come if you really 'live' them. For example, having your prepared statements pinned to a wall somewhere, or added to your promotional material, no matter how well written, achieves little or nothing. It is only by translating those broad sentiments into concrete goals, strategies and then plans that they can add value.

To make a lasting impact on your business, you therefore need to convert what you have written in these statements into measurable and time-bound strategic goals that will be used both to drive performance in the medium to long-term, but also to measure achievements along the way. These goals should again be stakeholder focused, so you could have a range of goals relating to:

Owners/ Investors	Finance, including return on investment, profitability, earnings per share, etc.
Customer	Goals should be defined around customers to include satisfaction and loyalty.

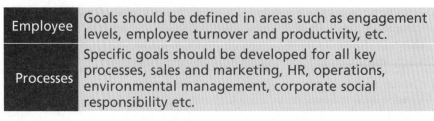

| Employee | Goals should be defined in areas such as engagement levels, employee turnover and productivity, etc. |
| Processes | Specific goals should be developed for all key processes, sales and marketing, HR, operations, environmental management, corporate social responsibility etc. |

By making your vision, mission and values more tangible through the creation of related strategic goals, you begin to bring them to life. Of course, there may be other business goals, but the strategic goals should be the overall driving force because they help to define *Where do we want to be?* as it applies to your business.

3. Strategy and Plans

As with any goals, the next step is to do something to achieve them, and this begins with strategy formulation. There is a lot of nonsense talked about strategy, but you must develop a strategy, or in reality a number of interlinking strategies, that will realise the goals you set. In other words, strategies begin to help you answer the question *How will we get there?* For example, if one of your strategic goals was to "increase customer loyalty levels by 40% within three years", then a clear strategy should be agreed as to how that particular goal is to be achieved. The same principles apply for all your goals, and if you had a financial goal like "to grow net profit to 15% within three years", you would also need to define a strategy to achieve that.

But, before you can do anything, it is simply not possible to develop any strategies or subsequent plans without insights; and insights come from having multi-source data to support decision-making. In other words, you need to really understand *Where are we now?* in relation to all aspects of the business before you start focusing on the *How will we get there?* bit. This, in part, involves looking internally at your strengths and weaknesses in terms of all aspects of business performance, such as financial, marketing, employees, products and services, etc. It also entails being externally focused and identifying opportunities and threats with regard to the economic environment, industry and market trends, customers, competitors and so on. You cannot devise strategy and plans if you don't know how you are performing at present. The questions covered in **Element 21** can be very helpful as you seek to develop your insights. Your strategies should help your business to play to your strengths, reduce the impact of any weaknesses, capitalise on opportunities identified and combat potential threats.

With general strategies agreed, the next important consideration is to ensure that you have, or can source, the necessary resources to bring strategy to life. Without appropriate resources, you don't have a viable strategy, but rather a wish list. And with resources defined, you then need to agree specific activities each year to translate those strategies into action. This requires some form of annual or tactical planning process that specifies which actions will be implemented in any given year so that you are executing your strategy.

It is through this integrated planning model that you can really answer the question *How will we get there?* and that is why all managers – and, where appropriate, employees – must understand the big picture and how their efforts contribute to achieving it.

4. Measure and Adapt

A key element in strategic management is of course concerned with measurement, and as a result you need continuous feedback to help you answer *How are we doing?* in terms of executing your plans, realising your strategies, achieving your goals and by correlation living by your values, implementing your mission and ultimately progressing towards your vision. And there are some important questions to be asked here.

How do You Measure Business Performance?

It's only fair to acknowledge that most businesses have become much better at measuring performance in the past decade or so, and many companies now use tools like The Balanced Scorecard, The EFQM model or The Performance Prism, which help to define broader measures of performance. These, and other, models encourage managers to view performance measurement in as wide a context as possible so that they truly understand how the business is doing as opposed to concentrating solely on financial metrics, which are critically important, but never tell the whole story. That said, and this particularly applies to small and medium-sized enterprises, the range and scope of performance measurement can still be too limited, and many businesses remain overly focused on the financial side of things. Non-financial measures such as customer satisfaction and employee engagement are also important and so too are measures of outputs from key processes such as IT, operations, marketing, HR, innovation, CSR and so on.

To really get to grips with the *How are we doing?* question, you therefore need a dashboard of measures which cover all aspects of business performance – financial and non-financial, customers, employees and so on to give you a holistic view of how the business is doing, particularly in terms of achieving your strategic goals. You should consider whether your current approach provides you with a real 360-degree view of how your business, or department, is performing at present.

Do You Have the Right Systems in Place to Provide the Information You Need?

Most businesses today have very strong financial information systems in place, but you might need to consider how effective your current approaches are in non-financial areas such as gathering customer or employee feedback. For example, a lot of customer-facing companies rely on comment cards to measure customer feedback but at best this hits only a very small percentage of overall customers and the information attained is also very limited. Yet, you hear managers all the time saying things like "We have 90% satisfaction rating from our customers." Maybe they do, but only based perhaps on 5–10% of their total consumer base and with regard to three or four aspects of the customer experience.

Do the Right People Get the Right Information Relevant to their Roles?

It is always important not to mistake quantity for quality in terms of the range and scope of measures you provide for your management team. The blanket approach, whereby all managers get the same data, can overload them and actually be counterproductive. Only give the right people the right information.

A related issue of concern here, and this is particularly relevant to more junior levels, is that, on occasion, some managers don't really understand the data they are presented with. As a result its use, in terms of supporting decision-making, is diminished. And, this issue is not just limited to junior ranks; for example, several CEOs in the major finance houses that failed in recent years later admitted that they didn't really understand the derivatives and other products that the quantitative analysts were devising, so a lot of the performance data they received meant little to them.

Do you Get that Information at the Right Time?

At what intervals do you currently take snapshot measurements in both financial and non-financial areas, and is that appropriate in a rapidly changing operating environment? Particularly, is what you currently do with the non-financial data sufficient? For example, many businesses only measure employee engagement once a year but this may not be sufficient as a lot can happen to motivation and commitment levels over the course of 12 months.

A second consideration here is the differentiation between measures that track *implementation* and those that focus on *impact*. If the agreed actions are not happening then you won't see the desired impact at a later stage, so you always want ongoing evidence that execution is actually taking place.

Are the Right Decisions Being Made with the Information You Have?

This has all to do with the effectiveness of decision-making that arises from the measurement information at hand. Key considerations here include asking who is involved in analysing the data and how good they are at it. It is important to ensure that you have a core team of managers – be that business-wide or at department level – with appropriate expertise across relevant dimensions who collectively review performance and make decisions accordingly. This analysis phase requires an investigation of root causes to ensure you are identifying the right issues and not just focusing on symptoms of more fundamental problems. Another consideration here is how you currently compare your results externally to determine how they stack up against industry norms and, more importantly, leading organisations.

The answers you come up with to these key questions should provide you with some food for thought in relation to how you currently measure ongoing and strategic performance across all dimensions of your business.

Here's a final thought on measurement. In *Corporate Governance Matters*, a book by two leading Stanford professors,[62] a case study is provided to highlight how managers of a fast food chain got things wrong. From their experience, the senior executives in the chain understood that customer satisfaction was an important driver of profitability and they 'knew' that low employee turnover was a key driver of satisfaction – so the managers used employee turnover as a key performance measure and as a result allocated a lot of resources to keeping that figure low. But, when they later received detailed performance results for restaurants across the chain, they found that some outlets with high employee turnover were amongst the most profitable and others with a lower turnover had poor profitability. Detailed statistical analysis of the results later showed that it was actually turnover amongst restaurant managers and not employees as a whole that made the difference to customer satisfaction and therefore to profitability. Are you sure you're measuring what matters most in your business?

There is no pretence that creating a winning strategy for your business is easy, but the strategic management process itself should not be so shrouded in complexity that only a few within the company actually understand it, or know how they can meaningfully contribute. It is a process that should involve everyone in the business, in a manner appropriate to their level and expertise, and strategic management should be part of what you do every day, not separate from it. In my experience, when strategy is something that only a few managers 'do', or when it's only discussed a couple of times a year, or at special strategic days or weekends, then that is problematic. Sure, you may have such formal strategy sessions at various intervals, but your strategies and plans should be a real part of day-to-day life within the business. Strategic planning and management should be the lens through which you view all aspects of your business and against which you hold all discussions or make all decisions.

And as you look through that lens right now, is the medium-term picture clear to you and everyone around you?

---

[62] Larcker and Tayan, *Corporate Governance Matters: A Closer Look at Organizational Choices and Their Consequences* (1st edition, Pearson Prentice Hall Pearson Education, Inc., Upper Saddle River, New Jersey 2011).

Managers Making Their Escape

Schettino: So, right now the ship is tilted …

De Falco: I understand that. Listen to me, there are people that are getting off using the rope ladder on the stern side, you go back there and you go up that ladder the opposite way, you go onboard the ship and you tell me how many people [are there] and what they need. You tell me if there are children, women or people that need assistance and you give me a number for each one of these categories, is that clear? Look Schettino, you may have saved yourself from the sea but this will put you through a lot of trouble, it will be very bad for you! Get back on board for [expletive]'s sake!

Schettino: Officer, please…

De Falco: There are no 'pleases'! Get back on board! Please assure me that you are going back on board…[63]

This is a short extract from the transcript of a lengthy radio conversation that occurred between Captain Francesco Schettino – the captain of the *Costa Concordia*, the cruise ship that ran aground and capsized off the coast of Italy, killing over 32 people – and Italian Coast Guard port official Gregorio De Falco. Now, we do know that allegedly attempting to sneak away from your sinking ship because you "tripped and fell into the lifeboat" (which has been widely reported as the excuse that Schettino gave for leaving the ship) is probably not a sign of a strong manager.[64] But if nothing else, Captain Schettino helped to remind us all that, regardless of context, those in charge need to deliver the goods at all times, particularly in a crisis. You may not be sailing ships around the Med for a living, but the issue of management effectiveness is just as important for you.

Recently when I was working with a number of managers, this issue of management effectiveness arose and I made the point that every manager should regularly assess his or her own effectiveness and that of other managers in their business so that they can continuously improve. That suggestion drew a sharp reaction from some in the group. It's not that those present around the table disagreed with the concept of measuring management effectiveness, but a number thought that the idea of doing so in a formal way was an unnecessary activity – great if they had little else to do, but a luxury for busy managers. One

[63] "Complete Transcript of Capt. Schettino and Italian Coast Guard Official", *New York Post,* 17 January 2012.
[64] Squires and Ward, "*Costa Concordia*: Captain 'Says He Tripped and Fell Into Lifeboat'", *Telegraph,*18 January 2012.

of the group reflected this view well when he said: "If my numbers don't stack up then I'll probably get the bullet from someone upstairs, and if my people aren't happy with how I manage them, then they'll mutiny or something, won't they? So why do I need to measure my effectiveness?"

And that's a fair point. After all, if you're not dismissed due to dodgy numbers, or if your people don't stage a revolt, then you can reasonably assume that you're effective, at least to some degree. Unfortunately, there are a couple of flaws associated with that viewpoint. First, striving to excel – which is something every manager should be doing – does not sit well with the notion of not knowing, or simply accepting things as they are; nor does waiting until it's too late to fix any problems. The quest for competitive advantage means constantly aiming to make all aspects of your business better in the spirit of continuous improvement, and that includes management.

Look at it another way. There isn't a manager on the planet who would disagree with the idea of measuring customer satisfaction levels because it's a known driver of business performance. Well, the same principle applies when it comes to management effectiveness – it drives results in your business, particularly today, and as a consequence needs to be monitored. And unless you have some concrete measure of management effectiveness, how can you ever hope to improve it? Additionally, just because employees don't openly revolt does not necessarily mean that they aren't unhappy, or that there aren't at least aspects of the way they are managed with which they have issues. If there are problems of that nature, isn't it better to know about them? To do that, you need to measure management effectiveness in a structured way.

And there are many ways to do so, ranging from the basic to the complex, but as a first step in seeking to measure management performance, you need to be specific about what you want your managers, at any level, to do in order for them to be described as 'effective'. For a long time, organisations relied solely on job descriptions for managers as the means to describe what they were expected to do, and whilst this is accepted practice, as mentioned elsewhere in this book, the major downside of job descriptions is that they focus more on what an individual is expected to do, as opposed to what they must achieve.

It is for this reason that developing some form of outcome-focused management competence model for your business is worth consideration if you don't have one already. Now, usually when I start talking to managers about competence models and the like, I can instantly see their eyes glaze over: "I'll leave that to HR if you don't mind." Despite the formal – and somewhat boring – undertones associated with the idea of a competence model, such a tool simply highlights the key areas that any manager should focus on, and more importantly it defines what they are expected to deliver in those areas. For this reason, they differ widely from one business to another; although what all managers should do is broadly similar, each organisation may want to prioritise different areas.

In setting out to devise a management competence model for your business or department, an early consideration is to define the key performance areas that matter most to you, making a direct link between your strategy and plans. Again, there are many ways to approach this but, in its simplest form all managers must deliver in relation to three critical areas: performance, people and process.

- *Performance* – achieving specific results in relation to their job, which may include maximising profitability, increasing sales, reducing costs, increasing customer satisfaction, reducing employee turnover and so on.
- *People* – achieving a whole range of outcomes in relation to their people, such as setting a positive example, communicating, motivating their team and handling conflict efficiently, to name a few.
- *Process* – achieving results in relation to the processes for which they are responsible, such as planning effectively, managing resources, providing training, sustaining quality and so on.

By focusing on these three areas, you can devise competences within each, and more importantly you can start to specify the results you expect in terms of each competence. Here's an extract to show what a simple competence model might look like:

			Sample criteria to define management effectiveness
Perfor-mance	→	*Define criteria that are related to meeting specific performance targets*	→	*Specific measures and targets could be defined for managers which might include an ability to meet:* ▪ Revenue targets ▪ Cost percentages ▪ Customer satisfaction ratings for their area ▪ Employee turnover in their area ▪ Number of accidents in their area ▪ Training hours provided to staff, etc.
People	→	*Develop criteria that are related to a manager's ability to lead others*	→	▪ *Self-motivated* and sets a positive example for employees in terms of attitude and performance ▪ Demonstrates high levels of *energy, enthusiasm* and *professionalism* ▪ Shows *concern* for team members and interacts with them in a positive manner

- Treats all team members *equally* and *fairly*
- Applies flexible *management styles* and regularly shows an ability to adjust their approach to deal with different people and situations
- *Communicates* in a structured and effective manner with people
- Builds and sustains effective *relationships* with employees and customers
- *Motivates* others to improved performance.

| Process → | Develop criteria that are related to a manager's ability to get the work done to a high standard → | - Demonstrates *commitment* to the company's vision and mission
- Understands their *roles* and *responsibilities* and demonstrates high levels of competence
- Continuously *develops* their own skills and knowledge
- Effectively *plans* and *organises* the workload in their department/area
- *Manages resources* to achieve the objectives agreed for their area
- Provides clear *direction* and *guidance* to their employees
- Ensures that work in their area is consistently carried out to the *standard* required
- Constantly strives to improve overall *quality* and promotes *continuous improvement* in their area
- Addresses *underperformance* in a proactive and constructive manner |

- Adopts a structured approach to *training, coaching and mentoring* their team
- Provides regular constructive *feedback* to employees
- *Solves problems* and shows initiative in finding creative solutions to work-related problems.

Clearly, the achievement of some of these outcomes is more easily measured, as they relate to hard data, whereas others are less tangible and would be assessed through a manager's annual appraisal, or from the results of the employee engagement survey completed by his or her employees. Therefore, as far as is possible, your management appraisal forms and the headings in your employee engagement survey must be closely aligned with those in whatever competence model you adopt, in order to facilitate the measurement process.

Naturally, it will take some time to get the system for measuring management effectiveness right in your business, particularly if you have nothing in place already, but it's worth the effort. And I'll leave you with this thought. A captain who skulks away from his ship has clearly failed the management challenge; no measurement of effectiveness is required there. However, in everyday life in your business, failures of management will rarely be so obvious. In fact, they can often go unnoticed but will still cause significant damage to performance somewhere along the line, either to the success of the manager in question, to that of his or her employees or to their section or department. And ultimately, your business will suffer as a result and that is something you definitely do not need just now when you have enough challenges to contend with.

So, it's worth asking yourself an important question: how do you spot managers making their escape within your business at present?

Never Standing Still

> "For the past 33 years, I have looked in the mirror every morning and asked myself: 'If today were the last day of my life, would I want to do what I am about to do today?' And whenever the answer has been 'No' for too many days in a row, I know I need to change something."[65]

I like that quote from the late Steve Jobs which he made as part of a commencement speech at Stanford University. Although, in that instance, he was referring to personal change, he was known to apply the same philosophy inside Apple too, so much so, that neither he nor the company ever stood still when he was in charge. When you look at all the various functions, activities and processes that make up your business, or area, you already know that there are lots of things that could be changed and improved over time. Indeed, as a manager at any level, you are already faced with constantly having to handle small and large changes alike. Although many of those changes are forced upon you by superiors, customers or competitors, you should, like Steve Jobs, never stop seeking out new and better ways of doing things so that you are both an instigator of change as well as an effective responder to it.

Given your existing experience of change, you will already know that especially where large-scale transformations are concerned the potential for problems is enormous, often beating the best of managers. This aspect of management performance – handling change that is – has received enormous attention over recent decades and you might imagine that the success rates in terms of positive outcomes from change programmes would be dramatically better as a result. But this does not seem to be the case at all and time and again studies show that change management failures are significant. In fact, the figure of a 70% failure rate is widely bandied about. One useful McKinsey & Company article reported on a survey where executives were asked to judge the success of change programmes in their business which for the purposes of the survey were defined as "a coordinated program, in companies or business units, that typically involves fundamental changes to the organization's strategy, structures, operating systems, capabilities, and culture."[66] The executives were asked to judge the effectiveness of their transformations based on two descriptions of success:

- One was how effective the change process had been in leading to improved profitability, return on capital employed, market value, and so on.

[65] Steve Jobs, Stanford University Commencement Address, 2005.
[66] Isern and Pung, "Organizing For Successful Change Management: A McKinsey Global Survey", (2006) June, *McKinsey Quarterly*.

- The second was how well the change process had "laid a foundation for sustaining corporate health over the longer term".

Based on the first metric, just 38% of respondents indicated that the transformation was "completely" or "mostly" successful at improving business performance, and on the second only about 30% were satisfied that the change process had improved their organisation's health and sustainability. About one-third of those managers surveyed also said they were "somewhat" successful on both counts in terms of key change processes. Worryingly, 10% indicated that they had been involved in change processes that were "completely" or "mostly" unsuccessful.

This is just one survey which shows that managers continue to struggle with the change issue. It should emphasise for you the need to pay very close attention to any such initiatives within your business, particularly those that are larger in scope, or require major surgery on how things are currently done. The bigger the upheaval, the more attention needed.

In my experience, a number of common problems arise when seeking to manage change, especially those of magnitude, and you should reflect upon the points ahead to consider how effectively you manage change at present.

Lack of Clarity about the Rationale, Purpose and Destination of the Change

This unfortunately is a common problem whereby a disconnect occurs between what George W would have called the 'deciders' of change and the 'implementers' of it. This gap can take a number of forms: sometimes, senior executives in the business are very clear as to why a change is necessary and what it should deliver, but there isn't the same degree of understanding at middle management level. Either they don't get the vision, or are not convinced of the need for change in the first instance. This is obviously problematic because it is ultimately that tier of management that is charged with executing the change. At times, the gap in understanding can exist between management and employees and this too can clearly create problems.

For change to succeed, or at least to raise the odds of success, from the outset all parties need to have a common understanding of why it is necessary and what the expected outcomes are likely to be. That is not to say that all will agree with, or indeed like, that rationale but they should at least be aware of it. And regardless of the nature of the proposals, change has to be 'sold' to some degree; sure, you can try to railroad changes through but that will only lead to significant overt and covert resistance. People do not like to feel powerless over issues that directly affect them. In addition, it is also important to highlight that change must lead to tangible benefits, if employees are expected to support it – where they don't see any positive outcomes you will always face an uphill struggle.

The Idea is Good, But the Execution is Poor

Even when a common vision for the change exists, and there is general support for it, its implementation can often falter due to failings across a number of interconnected dimensions:

- Lack of planning or organisation, which results in haphazard execution or insufficient resources to support the transition.
- The change process drags on too long, or stalls, and as a result the benefits aren't seen, which means that there's lots of pain, but little gain.
- Blockages that arise are not dealt with and employees lose faith in the new way of doing things. Such obstacles, if not quickly resolved, allow the resistors to claim the proposal is flawed and this can lead to a wider erosion of belief in and/or support for the desired changes.
- Communication is poor, leading to uncertainty and frustration; or in the absence of clear direction from managers the 'void' is filled by rumour or blatant misinformation by those opposed to the change.

Any change process is a project that must be managed and, as with any project, planning, organisation, leadership, communication and motivation are needed; in their absence, change processes will likely fail or at least under-deliver. In general, you should make sure that the implementation of any change process is time bound, as dragged-out change can be disheartening. Get the pain out of the way as quickly as is feasible. Also keep people actively involved in aspects of the initiative so they have things to do, or to contribute to the process. Don't have your people standing idly by watching the change happen – make them part of it.

Focusing Too Much on Process and Not Enough on People

Of course it is essential to address the issues raised above by having a structured approach to managing the change, with necessary plans, processes, timelines and resources in place to support the transformation. But too often, and despite this point being flagged frequently by change management experts, the people side of the equation is overlooked or at least not given the level of attention it deserves.

Reactions to change vary widely, and the culture within an organisation can play a role here too. Some people thrive on it, others are wary but willing, and there are those who can really fear and resist change. Often managers, who are generally more open to change in any case, can forget that employees have an attachment to the status quo, and therefore a vested interest in retaining it, and for them change represents a loss before it can ever lead to a gain. As a rule, times of change can be stressful and failing to deal with the natural human reactions associated with it can stymie progress.

An important point to recognise here too is the need to get the informal leaders onside as early as possible as they can help to bring other employees with them. Equally, watch out for any bad apples you might have around the place as they can have a field day, if you let them, during times of change. And this can apply regardless of whether the change process is viewed positively or negatively by the main body of employees; disgruntled individuals see that change initiatives, by their very nature, create uncertainty, and even fear, and this represents an opportunity for them to disrupt implementation, or at least create unnecessary hurdles. As an example of this potential problem one US internet services company recently found that a number of its clients' accounts had been hacked and information such as passwords altered, leading to widespread service disruption. After investigating the matter, senior management found that the source of the problem was not external as expected, but rather had been caused by an unhappy employee who was upset at a change initiative taking place within the company.

Taking Your Eye off the Ball

Change takes time to really bed in, and a common fault with many initiatives is that they receive a lot of management attention at the outset, but that can slowly wane with time as focus is drawn elsewhere. A change process is never compete until employees and other stakeholders see it as the norm, are fully committed to it and have long since left the 'old way' behind. For a big change, that could take years to achieve and you need to stick with a transformation process until the very end if you really want it to have the desired impact.

I think you will agree that the above are common challenges that arise when seeking to implement change of any kind – there are many more – and such issues can be magnified as the scale of transformation increases.

To conclude, the points addressed here on change management may be straightforward in principle, but based on the available research on the success rate of change initiatives, clearly something frequently goes astray in companies during times of change. Therefore, given that change is a prominent feature of business life these days, with that trend set to continue, in order to maximise the potential for success of your efforts in this regard, you should reflect upon how you can agree and follow a coherent approach to change management that addresses commonly identified failings, yet remains flexible enough to deal with evolving issues. In addition, by thinking more about the human side of things, you will be in a better position to sell change in a positive way, to anticipate likely problems and proactively respond to them. Focusing on the twin 'process-people' dimensions of managing change will increase your chances of attaining favourable results. And apart from dealing with changes that are imposed upon you, in conjunction with your people, you should always be on the lookout for ways of improving what you do, so that you are never standing still.

Winning isn't Everything, Why do They Keep Score?

You may be familiar with the Red Queen character from Lewis Carroll's *Through the Looking Glass*. For those not in the know, the Red Queen was the character that ran hard but never seemed to get anywhere because everything else in the landscape was also moving at pace. As she tells Alice, "It takes all the running you can do to keep in the same place!"

'What is all this about?', you are probably asking.

I am setting the scene for something which has become known in business life as the 'Red Queen Effect', whereby a lot of companies are forever running very fast but not really achieving competitive advantage, because when one company in the market does something new or different its competitors quickly catch up, so nobody really stands out. As I was recently reminded of this effect, it got me thinking about competition in general, and so the focus here will be on high-lighting some points about how you compete as a business, which could well be attributed to common sense, but they are no less important because of that.

1. Ignore Competition at Your Peril

The first point is a no-brainer in that you cannot ignore your competition. To do so has the potential to destroy even the best of businesses, so it's vital never to become complacent. The well-known and respected Harvard professor, Clayton Christensen, makes a very interesting point in his recent book[67] about what he refers to as the 'trap of marginal thinking'. As an illustration of this, he uses the well-known company Blockbuster and describes how they once dominated the movie rental business.

You could say that Blockbuster held all the aces at one point, particularly in the US where they had the biggest chain of nationwide stores, the largest inventory, the greatest purchasing power and so on. The key to their success was, however, not the number of videos it had on its shelves, but obviously how often those videos were rented out – only when a customer rented a movie did Blockbuster make money. They were pretty good at getting customers to rent videos and all seemed rosy in the garden. Then, out of nowhere, along came a company called Netflix with a new approach. Rather than make people go to the video store, they decided that they would mail DVDs to customers. In some ways their

[67] Christensen, *How Will You Measure Your Life?* (HarperCollins 2012).

business model was almost the reverse of Blockbuster. Netflix charged a monthly fee and as a result made money when customers didn't rent videos because they retained the fee but didn't incur delivery and collection costs.

Instead of taking Netflix seriously, Blockbuster totally underestimated the threat, and Christensen quotes one spokesperson for the company as having said: "We have not seen a business model that is financially viable in the long term in this arena. Online rental services are 'serving a niche market'." To cut a long story short, by 2011 Netflix had almost 24 million customers. And Blockbuster? Well, it declared for bankruptcy around that time and has since been bought out.

Sure, the market has dramatically changed now, with online provision a key factor, and there is probably room for store- and web-based options, but there is a moral to this story: failing to recognise and respond to competition is deadly, particularly when that competitor has dramatically changed the market dynamics. There are many such examples where established companies initially underestimated the potential impact of a new competitor which led to those incumbents being caught completely off-guard – think how Ryanair, Amazon, Dell and many other companies completely transformed how their industry, or segment, operated, and the length of time it took the established players to recognise that the ground had shifted from under their feet.

You cannot ignore your competitors, and this applies even if they are not radically changing the industry dynamics. Having said that, you also need to give a lot of thought to how you respond to what your competitors are doing.

2. Think Hard About Your Response to Competition

When you examine most markets, one of the frequent responses you see between competitors is to copy the good ideas the other introduces. Now, don't get me wrong, this can on occasion be the right move, depending upon the circumstances, but it can also frequently be the completely wrong option. For example, in the airline industry, when the likes of Ryanair first came along in Europe, think about how many of the established European airlines initially tried to copy the low-cost model, with little success. This is just one example of where the common response of 'follow the leader' in a competitive sense proved to be the wrong thing to do. Today, and after much wasted investment too, many airlines have long figured this out and companies such as British Airways, having at first tried to enter the low-cost arena through a separate arm, are instead seeking to put distance between themselves and the low fares model by focusing on quality, service and the overall flying experience offered.

On this issue of how companies compete, Joan Magretta, a senior associate at the Institute for Strategy and Competitiveness at Harvard Business School, makes the case that much of the competition within industries is about winning, or being the best,[68] but this is flawed thinking because, as she quotes Michael Porter, a leading expert on strategy and competition: "This is absolutely the

[68] Magretta, "Stop Competing to Be the Best", *HBR Blog Network*, 30 November 2011, at http://blogs.hbr.org/cs/2011/11/stop_competing_to_be_the_best.html

wrong way to think about competition. In fact, it's practically a guarantee of mediocre performance. The first problem with the competition-to-be-the-best mindset is that, in the vast majority of businesses, there is simply no such thing as 'the best'."

Magretta explains that there cannot really be any such thing as 'the best' in most industries because customers look for different things, or as she explains "the best hotel for one customer is not the best for another. The best sales encounter for one customer is not the best for another. There is no best car. There is no best art museum." Therefore, thinking only of trying to be the best, and competing on that basis alone, is problematic for managers, she argues, because:

> When rivals all pursue the 'one best way' to compete, they find themselves on a collision course, trapped in a destructive, zero-sum competition that no one can win. Everyone in the industry follows the same advice. Companies benchmark each other's practices and products. Customers, lacking meaningful choice, buy on price alone. Profitability deteriorates.[69]

What's the alternative then? Magretta returns to Porter for guidance and he urges that managers should strive to compete to be unique. Doing so, he argues, requires innovation not imitation and when you give people real choice then price is but one factor in the decision-making process. He suggests that "nothing is more absurd – and yet more widespread – than the belief that somehow you can do exactly what everyone else is doing and yet end up with superior results."

The lesson here? Keep an eye on your competitors, but do not necessarily 'do what they do'. And as you plan your competitive strategies and responses, one option could always be not to compete at all.

3. The Potential for 'Coopetition'

Imagine that you and an accomplice have just been arrested on suspicion of committing a serious crime, like a robbery. Each of you blames the other for the botched attempt. You are taken to the police station and held in separate rooms. You know that the police don't have enough evidence to charge you yet because you weren't actually caught red-handed, but you also know that there is no way you want to go to prison, not even for a single day.

After a while, a detective enters the room and makes the following proposition. "You have two choices," he begins "you can either choose to confess or keep schtum. If you confess and that idiot friend of yours next door stays quiet, then I will drop all charges against you, and she will do some serious time. And the opposite applies too, if she confesses and you stay silent, then she will walk and you'll do the time." He pauses for a moment to let that option sink in. Then he continues. "If both of you confess, then you'll both do time, but I'll make sure that you get a reduced sentence, say six months." He eyeballs you as he speaks those words. He then gives you another final option. "If you both refuse to talk, then I will only be able to charge the pair of you with acting suspiciously near the scene of a crime,

[69] *Ibid.*

which would probably mean a one-month sentence each and that would likely be suspended." He tells you he has made the same offer to your accomplice. Then he leaves you to stew for a while. Which option would you choose?

You may be familiar with that particular scenario. It's known as the 'Prisoner's Dilemma' and there are many versions of it floating around. It is often used to highlight, amongst other things, the tensions that arise between self-interest and the greater good. You will likely have figured out that, in the ideal world, by both keeping quiet, you each get a token sentence and walk. In other words, by cooperating, you can get the best result for *both* parties. But, in the real world, and seeing as you blame your accomplice for the failed robbery in the first place, plus the fact that you fear going to prison, you are most likely to try and outsmart her, and in attempting to do so the safest option is therefore to confess. But, highly likely, she will also figure that out too, so the probable outcome is that you'll both confess and end up doing six months – more time than you would have done had you cooperated.

That's a very short synopsis of the Prisoner's Dilemma, but it does help to flag some issues about cooperative versus competitive strategies. I am all for competition, but only when it's what I call 'positive' competition, and in line with the points made earlier about forging your own path. Consider it from two angles:

What negative competition can do to us as individuals: We often hear it said that "competition brings out the best in us". It does, but only when the 'smart' tag is attached to it. That means when competition is for competition's sake alone, it can actually bring out the worst in us, especially if we develop a win-at-all-costs mentality. It's not an exaggeration to say that some people lose the run of themselves when the competitive streak takes over.

What negative competition can do to organisations: Now, when there is no competition that's clearly never a good situation. Still, organisations too can suffer from the effects of bad competition and this can have serious consequences, particularly as alluded to earlier when 'winning' becomes more important than 'excelling', or when the rules become irrelevant in the face of the desire to outperform competitors, or the market as a whole. We only have to look at what happened in the banking and other sectors over recent decades when competition was based on short-term gains alone, or centred upon 'outperforming the other guy' as opposed to what was in the best long-term interests of stakeholders. You should also think internally here, particularly if you are in a large organisation, because often there are internal divisions leading to negative competition between departments which can affect business performance.

So, competition is good when smart, and it is smart when it leads to long-term added value, makes us – as individuals, organisations and customers – feel better not worse and when it delivers outcomes other than beating someone, or something, else. Still, even with those qualifiers attached, there are times when cooperating is actually the better option over competing and, yes, even in the cut-throat world of business; you should look more closely at where you might 'cooperate to compete'.

The idea of 'coopetition' – a term coined by Ray Noorda, the founder of Novell – is not a new one, but there are often potential advantages of combining both competition and cooperation strategies. For example, this already happens in many sectors:

Hospitality: As a simple case, think of food courts where a number of restaurants are located together in a single space sharing equipment, hygiene and cleaning services, etc. The approach brings the consumer to one location but allows them to decide between the various options available.

Retailing: Look at how Amazon works closely with other retailers and producers such as Toys R Us, Target, and Office Depot to name a few. Amazon provides sales platforms and distribution networks for a fee, and the participating companies gain exposure to Amazon's massive customer base.

Car Industry: Take the arrangement between PSA Peugeot and Toyota to share components for some models, in fact there are lots of similar examples across the motor industry.

Software: Even Google and Apple, at times sworn enemies, can still join forces when it suits them for mutual benefit and an example of this was how they were jointly involved in a group which purchased Kodak patents in 2012.

So, 'coopetition' is hardly a new concept, but the reality is that businesses by and large have only scratched the surface on this issue. It's hard to see beyond the competitive streak sometimes. As a consequence, think about where you might increase the potential for coopetition with others over the months and years ahead, through:

Sharing skills and expertise – when you come together with a competitor, you create a mix of skills and expertise which makes the whole stronger than the individual parts; all you need to do then is to define ways in which you can use that extra strength for mutual benefit.

Reducing Costs – as an example, by their very nature, many competitors in the same field use similar raw materials and inputs, it's what they do to turn them into outputs that differentiates the companies involved. But there is always scope for you to join forces with others to bulk purchase, or negotiate better terms from suppliers.

Joint Marketing – of course there are always rivalries between competitors in terms of gaining the bigger slice of the pie. That said, it is in both parties' interests if you can market together with a competitor in a way that makes the pie bigger. That's good for everyone.

Pooling backroom functions – activities such as administration, for example, are undoubtedly important, but rarely do they give a firm any competitive advantage. So there is nothing to stop you from pooling those functions, or other non-critical activities, even with direct competitors.

I could go on, but you likely get the point: the scope for coopetition is broad and is one possible option worth considering for how you can grow in a competitive market.

The main points to remember are that, now more than ever, you must be aware of what's happening in terms of competition, but you also need to be clever in how you respond. Before deciding upon the best route forward, ask yourself whether 'doing what they do' is the appropriate response in terms of your overall vision for your business. As an alternative strategy, think about how you might find clear blue water by completely differentiating your offering from what others are doing, or putting distance between your business and the rest of the pack. And even more radical, maybe the best route forward on occasion is to cooperate, not compete. Sometimes we are unintentionally blind to opportunities because we get hung up on winning, as the title of this Element – a quote from the legendary coach Vince Lombardi – suggests.

Sure, it can mean everything, but then again, that depends upon how you define winning.

It 's Good to Hug

"We hug trees."
"Ha-ha, very funny," I replied.
"We hug trees and, oh yes, we recycle paper," he added, which got a big laugh from those around the table. They were all finding this hilarious indeed. Nothing it seems brightens up the day more, for some people at least, than winding up the consultant. Glad to be of service, I suppose.

I was discussing the issue of 'Corporate Social Responsibility' (CSR) with a business owner and his senior team and that's how he kicked off his answer to my enquiry about what they were already doing in this general area. Despite his button-pushing he usually has some valuable insights into various aspects of business life, even if it's often necessary to wade through a fair helping of sarcasm to find them. During the discussions we touched upon more serious matters in relation to CSR. Like most companies these days, he has some initiatives in place which fall under that broad umbrella – mainly, in this case, related to energy and waste management, all fairly standard stuff really. Truth be known, he does them more because he has to – recent legislation gives him little choice on the matter – rather than out of any great zeal for CSR.

His own words on the subject are worth considering. "Look, we do our bit to save the planet, but apart from the feel-good factor for some of the team, I find it very hard to figure out whether all this CSR palaver actually pays-off in terms of the bottom line. Yes, we saved a fair bit on our energy and waste bills since we made the changes, but those savings were only really seen in the first year or two. They've pretty much levelled off now … is it really worth all the hassle?"

He is far from alone on that score; similar opinions on the matter are widely expressed by managers in both large and small businesses alike. Worse still, some companies seem to use CSR more as a PR tool than a true strategic business driver to the point where it's often described as 'greenwashing' – that is, pretending to be environmentally friendly for the sake of appearances. But there is mounting evidence that when companies really do buy into CSR it can make a big difference in performance, so the focus here is to get you to think about how to maximise those benefits in your business.

1. What is CSR and Why Bother with it?

First off, let's start with a quick snapshot of what we mean by CSR, because there is often a degree of uncertainty about what it entails. In reality, it is not possible for any business to conduct its activities in isolation from a range of stakeholders such as employees, customers, society, government and so on, and CSR is essentially a catch-all term that describes how a business interacts with those stakeholder groups, for everyone's benefit. Mallen Baker,[70] a writer, speaker and strategic advisor on corporate social responsibility, has designed a practical model that helps to bring all the stakeholders in terms of CSR together:

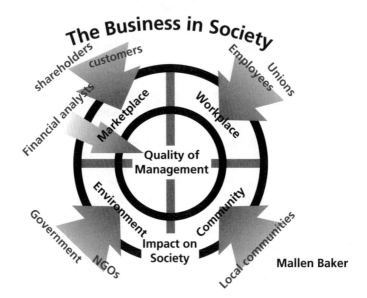

This diagram summarises very well the multitude of potential stakeholder interactions any company can have in conducting its business and how the focus should be to try to 'do the right thing' by all of them: from ethical dealings with consumers, to fair treatment of employees, to positive interaction with the local community and so on. In light of this, the range of activities that can help to build CSR within any business, large and small, is extensive and what can and should be done will naturally vary dramatically from one company to another. But why bother with CSR in the first place?

As indicated earlier, there is general scepticism about the benefits of CSR, but businesses that do focus on the issue as a strategic concern see a mix of returns, including:
- Lower costs and greater efficiencies
- Increased goodwill, customer loyalty and ultimately sales growth
- Improved employee retention, engagement and raised productivity
- Reduced reputational risk, or legal challenges resulting from bad or unethical business practices
- Improved access to capital and finance through CSR-focused investors or funds.

[70] See www.mallenbaker.net

These benefits do result from effective CSR and the evidence to support that assertion is mounting. However, measuring the precise impact of CSR on the bottom line, given that there is no model approach, is extremely hard, so there are conflicting opinions on the real level of impact. Still, there are plenty of concrete examples out there of successes in individual enterprises to indicate that strong CSR focus does makes an important difference, including:

- Marks & Spencer claims that its Plan A eco-programme made it an extra £50 million in 2010.[71]
- A US study of 3,000 grocery shoppers[72] showed that broad initiatives like environmental friendliness and community support build only goodwill, but initiatives like offering locally-sourced products and fair employee compensation – actions related directly to the products and people that consumers face – bring both goodwill and a higher share of wallet (level of expenditure per person) from consumers. The authors of the study showed that if a retailer is able to improve consumers' perception of its fair treatment of employees by one point on a five-point scale, the consequent increase in revenue is approximately 1.7%. The gain from a similar improvement in local sourcing is even more pronounced, at more than two percentage points. They argue that "these numbers appear small, but they represent a sales lift of 10% to 15% for the average retailer in our study."
- A Harvard University study[73] found that stakeholder-balanced (i.e. CSR-orientated) companies showed four times the growth rate and eight times the employment growth rate compared with shareholder-only focused companies.

Yes, it may well be difficult to prove without doubt the exact impact of CSR across the board on profitability because not every company does the same thing, so it's hard to compare like with like, but there are clearly strong correlations between CSR and improved business performance. Without a doubt, the issue deserves your attention, even – if not more so – during these difficult times.

2. How to Get the Most from CSR in Your Business

As with any aspect of business operation, what you get from CSR will depend upon what you put into it. And what you put into it will be influenced by many factors such as the size, type and location of your business. A simple conceptual framework for applying CSR in any business entails:

Commitment

Before anything else, CSR is all about a way of thinking. If the management team in any given business truly believe in it then there is no shortage of practical

---

[71] "Doing the Right Thing: Our Plan A Commitments 2010–2015", Marks & Spencer Group PLC. See http://corporate.marksandspencer.com/documents/publications/2010/planacommitments2010

[72] Ailawadi, Luan *et al*, "Does Retailer CSR Enhance Behavioral Loyalty: A Case for Benefit Segmentation", Tuck School Working Paper, (Dartmouth College 2011).

[73] Kotter and Heskett, *Corporate Culture and Performance,* (Reprint edition 2011).

initiatives that can be taken which are good from a CSR point of view but also make sound business sense; the stronger that commitment, the greater the results.

Ask yourself:
- How committed to the concept of CSR are you at present in your business?
- How is that commitment shown and communicated?
- Are you leading or following in terms of CSR in comparison with your competitive set?
- Who's driving CSR strategically and operationally within your business?

CSR Assessment

A full CSR audit should frequently be carried out to help define *Where are we now?* in relation to CSR. As part of this, you should consult key stakeholders to determine their expectations; this is a really useful activity, particularly when it relates to consumers, because you can begin to determine how interested they are in CSR-related matters, what their expectations of you are in that regard and even whether they are willing to pay a premium in terms of the products and services you offer.
- Do you know what your customers (individuals and businesses) expect of you in terms of CSR, beyond the generic concerns? Are you delivering on those expectations?
- Apart from customer-focused initiatives, what other aspects of CSR are you working on in the business?
- How broad and effective are your employee engagement efforts?
- How environmentally friendly are you at present? Have you managed to make significant savings in recent years in areas like energy and waste management costs?
- Are your suppliers true partners in your business or do they just drop items off at the delivery bay or reception?
- How strong are your links with the local community, charities, schools and so on?
- What returns are you currently seeing for your CSR efforts? What more could you do across the spectrum of CSR activities?

CSR Policy

A general CSR policy that is simple, coherent, and fully communicated is helpful because it lets people (internal and external stakeholders) know what your CSR intentions are, and it also puts pressure on you to deliver once you go public with those intentions.
- What have you publicly committed to in terms of CSR at present?
- How broad are those commitments? Are you doing a little or a lot?
- Do you deliver what you have promised?
- If not, why not?

CSR Strategy and Plans

Of course, to bring the CSR policy to life, clear strategies and related plans are needed. Here's a simple exercise: in your own mind, list five concrete actions being consistently applied within your company this year that show there is a vibrant and meaningful CSR strategy in place.

Implementation and Impact

As with any strategy or plan, what really matters in the end is how well it is executed. Another reflection exercise:

- For one of the five actions you identified a moment ago, how well is that particular activity executed?
- What is the expected impact of that activity in terms of something measurable, such as reduced cost, lower risk, or increased sales, etc.?
- What has it actually delivered?
- Is there a negative performance gap? Why?

These are perhaps early-stage questions to consider in relation to building an approach to CSR but that doesn't make them any less important. In addition, don't make the mistake that CSR was a 'nice to have' during the boom years but is now surplus to requirements in a recession, or when the business environment remains challenging. Research shows that, regardless of trading conditions, when CSR is approached in a meaningful and consistent way within any business it can make a positive difference in terms of performance, even if at times it is hard to fully quantify what the bottom-line impact of those benefits are. As my client from earlier said to me as he walked me out at the end of my visit, finally admitting that, despite his sarcasm about tree hugging and all the rest, he could see the benefits of CSR to his business: "It's good to hug", he said with a smile as he turned and strode off having shook my hand. And I noticed how he stopped to switch off the unnecessary exterior light as he did so.

Ri pe for the Picking

"Sorry, we can't hear you at the back …".
Unmerciful screeching and audio feedback as adjustments take place.
"Is that any better?"
"No."
Eardrum-bursting screeching.
"How about if I just speak more loudly and don't bother using the micro-phone?"
A smattering of applause from those at the back of the room. Then the speaker begins what essentially amounts to shouting.
"Now, it's too loud at the front."
"What if I stand back over here?"
"We can't see the screen if you do that."

And so it went for the first 10 minutes or so, until they sorted out the sound problems. This happened at a conference organised by a local business school I attended recently. It wasn't the speaker's fault, and I felt very sorry for him. And the title of the conference? 'Innovation in Turbulent Times'. Innovation? How about figuring out how to work the microphones? That would be a good start. Sure, these things happen and you probably think that I must be a right old cur-mudgeon but I'm not – really – that little scenario just helps me set the scene for focusing upon the issue of innovation.

It's certainly not curmudgeonly to make the point that there is a lot of hype about innovation in every field. All businesses today, or certainly most, want to be portrayed as innovative – 'the learning organisation', and so on. Listen to any speech or read any article by a business leader and the word 'innovation' will undoubtedly figure at some point. According to the *Wall Street Journal*, "a search of annual and quarterly reports filed with the Securities and Exchange Commis-sion shows companies mentioned some form of the word 'innovation' 33,528 times last year, which was a 64% increase from five years before that."[74]

So, innovation is widely talked about, but is it a reality on the ground? One study, a report released by Capgemini Consulting and the IESE Business School,[75] provides some insights into the answer to that question. The study was based on a survey of 260 innovation executives from around the world and

[74] Kwoh, "You Call That Innovation? Companies Love to Say They Innovate, but the Term Has Begun to Lose Meaning", *Wall Street Journal*, 23 May 2012.
[75] Miller *et al.*, "Innovation Leadership Study. Managing Innovation: An Insider Perspec-tive", Capgemini Consulting and IESE Business School.

found that the innovation success rate in surveyed companies, as determined by "the percentage of innovation efforts that have a positive material impact on the company's business results" was as follows:

- 38% of respondents fit within the innovation laggard profile (less than 25% success rate)
- 7% belong to the innovation leaders group (over 75% success rate)
- 37% of companies had a success rate of 25–50%
- 18% showed a 50–75% success rate.

Additional findings from the report include that:

- 43% of respondents indicated that their companies did have a formally accountable innovation executive which was up from 33% the previous year
- Only 42% have an explicit innovation strategy
- Just 11% have a strategy that involves employees and not just executives in the strategy development process
- Only 30% agree that they have an effective organisation structure for innovation
- 39% say they do not have an effective decision-making process for innovation
- Only 24% of the respondents think they have an "effective organizational alignment of innovation efforts"
- 54% of survey participants indicate that they do not have a formal KPI system for promoting or measuring innovation.

These and other reports indicate that, although people like to talk about innovation, that doesn't always translate into meaningful action on the ground. Few managers argue against the need for it, but there remains work to be done to ensure that innovation becomes a defined and meaningful process in many companies and one that delivers measurable results.

Larger companies may well have a distinct R&D function, with appropriate staffing and resources, to drive innovation within the business. That's great if you have it, but the focus here will be on how innovation can be applied in smaller scale operations where the resources to support the process may be more limited and the ambitions less grand. Regardless of the nature of your business, to have an effective approach to innovation requires you to consider the process in **Figure 27.1**, below.

Before applying this process there are a couple of general issues to reflect upon when thinking about innovation. First off, you should clearly define your objectives for the process in your business. Now, it may sound counterintuitive to set boundaries for a creative activity, but by defining the areas of the business where you want to see improvements you can focus your innovation efforts and resources more efficiently. You cannot innovate for the whole business at once, so it's necessary to pick specific areas or processes where you see priority needs for improvement. In addition, if you attach goals or metrics for what you want to achieve (even activity-based ones, such as the number of new product or service ideas generated in the next period) this can later help to measure the effectiveness of your efforts at innovating.

Figure 27.1   **Managing innovation in small and medium enterprises**

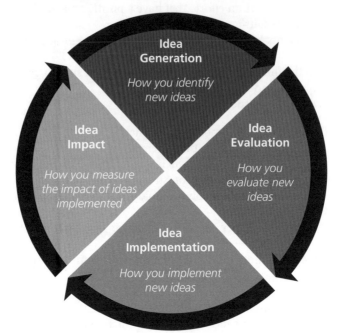

The second concern here is that before you do anything in this area, or even revise your existing approach, be aware that what really drives internal creativity and innovation is having managers and employees who are fully engaged with each other and the business. People need to have a real commitment to the company and a desire to be the best at what they do. Without this, the potential for new ideas will be limited or confined to the truly dedicated few. If you have engaged and motivated people, you will be surprised at what they come back with when challenged to identify new ways of doing things. If you don't have such employees, then you need to focus on that particular issue as a priority before you even start worrying about innovation.

1. Idea Generation

Ideas lie at the heart of innovation and generating them requires you to focus upon a number of key activities:

Create Internal Ideas Platforms

Although, as mentioned, engaged employees are a proven source of new ideas, as you seek to harness their support in this regard, it is important not to create the impression that coming up with ideas and suggestions is an optional activity, or something to be done outside of the 'normal' work routine. No, contributing ideas and suggestions is everybody's responsibility and should be the norm, not the exception. If you really think about it, a lot of companies unintentionally send out the wrong message when they make a fuss about internal idea generation in that they separate 'doing' from 'thinking'. You pay your employees for their brain as well as their brawn, and whilst you do need an innovation process to manage the flow of ideas, contributing suggestions should not be seen as a separate activity from what people do every day, but rather an integral part of it.

In terms of facilitating the gathering of ideas from employees, the suggestion box is widely adopted in many organisations. Yet I rarely see this model work all that well, and certainly not in the longer term. Too frequently the box ends up positioned in somewhere like the canteen where, over time, it can become a useful surface to rest empty cups on, or within which to deposit used sweet wrappers and the like – a monument to lost opportunity. When used correctly the suggestion box can form part of broader internal ideas platforms, but you do need to be creative in how you use it so that you keep it 'fresh'. Alternatively, idea-generation within your business could be structured as follows:

- As highlighted elsewhere in this book, heads of department (HODs) and other managers should be formally meeting with their employees on a monthly basis to discuss work-related matters, and as part of that meeting a section of the agenda could be devoted to employees submitting ideas and suggestions relevant to their area, or even for other parts of the business.
- All employees, either individually or in small teams, should then be required to come up with at least one new idea per month, no matter how small, and present it at the monthly meeting. That's hardly a big ask, is it? To generate one new idea every 30 days? To help focus employee thinking, you could designate some categories from within which ideas can be suggested, for example:
  ○ Ideas that help to maximise profitability;
  ○ Ideas that help to better engage employees;
  ○ Ideas that help to create memorable products/experiences for customers; and
  ○ Ideas that help to deliver operational efficiencies.
- In turn, each HOD would then attend the next senior management meeting and present the best of the ideas generated from within their department for consideration.

This approach would mean that there was a defined structure in place to facilitate the upward channelling of ideas in your business, and that idea-generation as an activity was also seen as part of working life, not separate from it. Another approach to internal idea generation could be to create cross-functional 'ideas teams', then focus their efforts as above, set them some targets, resource them and then let them off.

Listen to Your Customers

Of course, another great source of information about what you can do differently, or better, is your customers. By watching and listening to them in a structured way, you may identify opportunities to tailor what you do at present, create new products and services or even to build something entirely new.

Establish External Benchmarking Activities

Additional sources of new ideas are those that come from outside your business and naturally you need to stay in tune with what your competitors are doing, trends in your industry, changing needs and habits and so on. More formally, process benchmarking is also a vital component in stimulating innovation. 'Process benchmarking' essentially means picking a particular business process, let's say sales, or more likely specific aspects of it, and learning how leaders in your industry – and beyond – manage that particular aspect of the process. It involves building relationships, or partnerships, with companies that excel at the activity, arranging on-site visits to explore how they do it so well, learning the lessons, and adapting not adopting what they do to fit your business. It requires planning, resources and effort to develop meaningful benchmarking relationships.

There are other external avenues to explore in relation to garnering new ideas that are also worth considering. You may well have heard of 'Open Innovation' and 'Crowdsourcing' of late, wherein innovating is seen as something to be done in partnership with others outside your company, through an agreed process which shares the risks and rewards of the outcomes. There are many online platforms springing up that facilitate this open process. For example:

- *The Innovation Exchange*, which is an online open innovation marketplace.[76]
- *InnoCentive*, is an open innovation and crowdsourcing portal.[77]
- *ExploreB2B* is a social platform geared towards business professionals that enables people to share ideas, find future partners and utilise international talent and resources.[78]

I have no affiliation to any of these entities and they are merely intended as examples, amongst the many others out there, which are worth a look at in terms of how you might extend your innovation reach.

As you think about how you might involve people more (customers, employees and external partners) in your innovation process, bear in mind that famous quote by Henry Ford when talking about developing the Model T: "If I had asked people what they wanted, they would have said a faster horse." Finding truly innovative ideas by asking people what they want, or think, is a good idea but can also be somewhat limiting at times because their answers are generally shaped by their existing reference points. So, to limit this barrier, don't be afraid to really encourage people to think without fear or limitation and using brainstorming techniques can be helpful in this regard; encourage people to be as unfettered as they can be, and out of that freedom useful ideas can flow.

2. Idea Evaluation

Frequently, new ideas generated within a business disappear into a black hole somewhere and employees who do bother to contribute never hear anything back about their particular suggestion. This naturally demotivates them from coming up with suggestions in future. In any business, designated members of the management team should evaluate all the ideas presented each month, pick

[76] www.innovationexchange.com
[77] http://www.innocentive.com/
[78] https://exploreb2b.com/

the most feasible for implementation or further investigation, but ensure that all employee submissions are acknowledged in some way, so that people are motivated to continue suggesting ideas even if they aren't always successful in having them taken on. You should consider how you will manage the acknowledgement and evaluation of ideas submitted.

3. Idea Implementation

When a new (workable) idea is identified following your evaluation, how it will be implemented will naturally depend upon the nature and scale of the idea. However, there must be a structured approach in place to ensure that selected ideas are developed, launched and fully bedded down in the business, rather than falling into the trap of flavour-of-the-month syndrome, where there is often great excitement as a new idea is launched, but then over time it is forgotten. Naturally, employees who come up with selected initiatives should be involved in some way in their implementation too.

Many companies financially reward employees for ideas implemented but, against the conventional wisdom, I don't think that's a smart idea at all. Financially rewarding employees for coming up with ideas – even if implemented – again sends out the wrong message that 'thinking' is something special or separate from what they should be doing anyway. Maybe in exceptional circumstances if an employee's idea saved, or made, you a fortune, that might be different, but as a rule I would not reward ideas financially.

That said, every idea implemented must be 'rewarded' in the sense that the employee(s) concerned should be recognised and publicised internally for their contribution – and gifts can of course be appropriate in that context. In addition, such positive behaviour should also be recognised in terms of appraisals, salary reviews and, naturally, those employees who consistently contribute most in this regard would – all other things being equal – jump up the list for promotion, if that's on their agenda.

4. Idea Impact

As with any business activity, you want to know if you are getting better at it, so performance measures should be defined for the innovation process. These can track *implementation* (such as the number of new ideas implemented per annum) or *impact* (such as savings made as a result of a new idea introduced or process tweaked). It's vital to know what the process is delivering for your business.

Innovation is undoubtedly much hyped but it is a vital business activity nonetheless, particularly today when finding new and better ways of doing things is a necessity. By considering these four phases of innovation as they apply to your business and then better structuring your innovation process in response, you do not kill creativity but rather, over time (and if adhered to), will make people realise that innovation is part of what they do, not something to be done every now and again, or when a problem arises. The words of A.G. Lafley, Former

CEO of Procter & Gamble (P&G) resonate here when he said "Innovation is P&G's lifeblood. Without it we will fail. The P&G we're trying to unleash today asks all 100,000-plus of us to be innovators. We actively solicit new ideas, and if the concept is promising, we put it into development."

Finally, too often innovation is portrayed as a quest for the next big thing, and this can be true in some enterprises or fields, but more of the time it's about finding those thousands of little ideas that are ripe for picking.

All Persons Ought to Endeavour to Follow What is Right and Not What is Established

Take a look at the picture below:

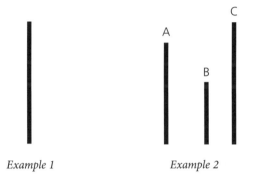

Example 1   *Example 2*

Now, answer this simple question: which of the three lines in Example 2 on the right matches the length of the line in Example 1 on the left? Not a particularly hard question I'll admit and undoubtedly you identified C as being the best match. But, think again, are you sure that's the right answer? Look very closely once more ... Is there any way that I, or anybody else for that matter, could convince you to change your mind, and maybe pick B or A as the best match?

No, sticking to your guns on C, are you?

You would imagine that's what everyone would do when faced with this particular problem: stick to their guns that is, especially when the answer is clear. And it's definitely C, so why would anyone ever change their mind? Or so you would think, but that's not necessarily the reality of the matter. In a classic set of social experiments conducted by a psychologist named Solomon Asch back in the 1950s, known as the Asch Experiments,[79] when shown the same or similar pictures as those above, 75% of people actually denied their own senses at least once, and chose either A or B as the answer – even when they knew that to be wrong. How could anyone, never mind such a large number of people, do that? Here's some background on how and why it happened.

[79] Asch, "Effects of Group Pressure Upon The Modification and Distortion of Judgment", in Guetzkow (ed.) *Groups, Leadership and Men* (Carnegie Press 1951).

Asch selected 12 participants for his test and brought them one at a time into a room where up to eight others were already seated around a table, and he introduced them as fellow participants in the experiment. The group were then shown the above picture (or similar) and asked the same question: which line – A, B or C – was the same length as the reference line on the left? This procedure was repeated 12 times with participants viewing variations of the above picture.

What the 12 selected participants didn't realise was that all others in the room were actually playing roles agreed with Asch in advance. They had been told to give the wrong answer to the question. On half of the trials they called out the line that was too short as being the match, and on the other half the line that was too long. In advance of the tests, Solomon Asch believed that the majority of selected participants would not go along with something so obviously incorrect, but it turned out he was wrong; when faced with a group who seemed to accept the wrong answer, 75% of the selected participants gave an incorrect answer to at least one question.

These findings received a lot of attention at the time and subsequently have led to many similar studies which consistently show the impact of peer pressure and conformity on group interactions. As with any aspect of human behaviour it is undoubtedly a very complex area and, at the risk of over-simplifying things, it can be said that many people prefer to adapt to the norm rather than to stand out from the crowd. This social pressure to fit in comes easily to some, but can often produce strong feelings of internal conflict in others yet they still conform. Others of course find it easy not to follow the herd but they have been shown to be in the minority.

You are probably wondering what this has to do with daily work. Well, it's surprisingly relevant. This brief summary of the Asch experiments raises the issue of conformity and its potential implications for the workplace. On the one hand, a degree of conformity is naturally required in any work situation whereby we create an environment within which everybody is expected to abide by a set of written and unwritten rules. There's nothing necessarily wrong with that, as no organisation could function efficiently if everybody was allowed to do their own thing. Obviously, the acceptable levels of toeing the line found in Google offices for example will be very different from those seen in a government department. So, conformity is not a bad word once it doesn't turn into blind obedience.

However, it can have negative consequences and one such example is described as 'groupthink', defined in research by Yale psychologist Irving Janis as occurring "when a group makes faulty decisions because group pressures lead to a deterioration of mental efficiency, reality testing, and moral judgment".[80] The issue of groupthink has been widely discussed ever since Janis's work and it is now an accepted phenomenon.

I have seen plenty of examples of it in action in organisations large and small and groupthink often occurs in circumstances where people become so focused on achieving consensus that opposing views or alternative proposals are overlooked and even subtly discouraged – in other words, they go with the flow.

[80] Janis, *Groupthink: Psychological Studies of Policy Decisions and Fiascoes* (Houghton Mifflin 1983).

For example, working in one client organisation it was manifest in hc group of senior managers and owners collectively convinced themselves 'their' strategy or approach was the best way forward even when faced with mounting evidence that a change of course would have been the better option. Yet, when speaking individually to some of those involved, it was clear that they didn't wholly buy into the existing approach, but felt they had to go along with it as they didn't want to appear 'out of step' with the boss. I have also seen examples of a form of groupthink further down the chain of command, where individuals within a team or department are swayed in their views by one or two stronger characters, often to the point where they end up publicly supporting a stance that they don't actually agree with.

Groupthink is unlikely to be an issue you give a whole lot of thought to on a daily basis, but it's worth reflecting upon your own organisation or department for a moment to consider what, if any, instances of groupthink there may be. The propensity for conformity of thought increases when certain factors are present:

- If the manager of a work group is a very dominant, authoritarian or aggressive character who directly or indirectly lets it be known what particular outcome he or she wishes to achieve on any given matter.
- When a team is very close (and closed) and there is a desire to put the needs of the group ahead of the wider needs of the business.
- When there is too much emphasis placed on harmony and a track record has built up of not rocking the boat; people within that team come to understand that dissenting voices are not necessarily welcome.
- Where one, or a number of individuals, as in the example above, play strong informal leadership roles in a team, this can lead to the majority going along with the views of the few. By the way, this can be achieved through subtle influence as well as outright bullying.
- Where large numbers of individuals within a team are apathetic or disengaged and simply go along with whatever is agreed just because that requires the least energy.

Whatever the causes of groupthink, as a manager you need to be aware of it because when present it leads to poor decision-making, lack of creativity, and even unvented disgruntlement, as some people go along with things they don't really agree with. To prevent groupthink, you can take some simple steps:

- Avoid exercising undue influence over the decision-making process on any particular issue, especially at early stages when opinions are not yet formed. By all means frame the problem at hand but encourage people to explore alternative solutions and leave your own opinions out of it for as long as you can.
- Use external experts and facilitators for really important decision-making processes such as strategy development. They can help to widen the debate and discussion and reduce the potential for groupthink.
- Have clearly defined processes or structures for making decisions which, as a minimum, require you to evaluate more than one option or solution.
- Promote views dissenting from the norm. Always encourage your people to counter-argue against proposals. You can do this in little ways by asking questions such as: *can anyone pick a hole in what was just proposed?*

- Use individual job-chats and formal appraisals to get a better handle on what the various personal viewpoints are within the team.
- When you hear team members, particularly those you know are the informal leaders, using terms such as 'we' to describe how the group feels, be conscious that they may well be referring to how they, or a small number of staff, feel, but not the group as a whole.

None of the above points are dramatic actions in themselves, but reducing the potential for groupthink doesn't require grand gestures. What is needed is an acceptance that it is a real and potentially damaging phenomenon that is frequently overlooked by managers. During challenging times, when difficult and often fundamental decisions need to be taken, which directly affect the future of the business and its employees, it is essential that such vital decisions are not influenced by groupthink, or that dissenting, and alternative, voices are not crowded out during the decision-making process. And the issue of groupthink is far from a new concern either, because for as long as people have assembled in groups, its dangers have been known, as evidenced when Aristotle said: "All persons ought to endeavour to follow what is right, and not what is established ..."

Project Red (Faced)

The supermarket close to where I live here in Geneva nearly faced a riot not so long ago. Well, I am not entirely sure that it's possible to classify what happened as a riot, seeing as it was mostly a gang of seniors involved. What caused all the shenanigans? Well, it all revolved around a new competition they were running. Prior to its launch, I had noticed that the place was suddenly swamped with posters and point of sale displays signalling the imminent arrival of a new in-store Lotto-type game for shoppers spending over a certain amount. It turned out to be a disaster.

The crux of the game was as follows. Depending on how much you spent on your shopping, you received a certain number of slips that looked like lotto tickets, with a big bar-code on the front. Then, you had to queue again in a different part of the store and wait your turn to scan your ticket in an over-sized machine which looked like something out of a Las Vegas casino. Once you scanned your ticket, this triggered a hullabaloo of lights and fruit machine music, culminating, after 10 seconds or so, in a big flashing sign indicating whether you had won something or not, and the amount won if you had been successful. It was one of the most ridiculous things I have ever seen.

That said, I do enjoy the way people lose the run of themselves when the chance of winning money is on the cards, so I decided to stick around for a while and watch things unfold. First off, the machine crashed after the first few people had used it: no lights, sound or action of any sort which in turn triggered the arrival of a swarm of young MBA manager-types who all ended up staring into the back of the machine, none of them seemingly having the slightest clue what they were looking for. Then, shortly afterwards, following some serious walkie-talkie action, the ubiquitous man in blue overalls arrived. He fiddled a bit at the back for a while and that seemed to sort things out.

Meanwhile, the queue had grown significantly, in length and impatience. Next problem was that, after a few more goes, one lady scanned her ticket but nothing happened. She scanned it again and again but still nothing. Then, she left the queue to complain. Meanwhile, the woman who was next in line stepped forward, scanned her ticket and low-and-behold won 500 Swiss Francs. Cue mayhem.

The first lady went back over to the machine and insisted that the prize should be hers, whereas the winner obviously wasn't having any of it. They started screaming at one another, each trying to grab the prize receipt that was printed out (by the way, to claim the prize meant queuing a third time at the customer service desk). Meanwhile, others behind them in the queue were now yelling for them to move on. Shoppers were stopping for a look. A crowd was gathering. The store manager came upon the scene and before he knew it he was surrounded by what seemed to be 10 or 15 little old ladies and a couple of men, in various stages of rage; one of them even took a swipe at him with her hand-bag. Store security and, ridiculously, even the police arrived on the scene a while after – I had visions of them cuffing all the seniors and lining them up outside.

There were undoubtedly a lot of red faces at the next store management meeting as they tried to figure out how things went so badly wrong. Oddly enough, the whole incident got me thinking about project management. Now, I'll be the first to admit that I'm no expert on project management, but I have managed many projects in the past, of various sizes, and indeed have seen – as you probably have – projects fail on occasion. Regardless of your role, level or indeed industry, project manage-ment will be an important aspect of what you do as a manager. Of course, I am not talking here about things on the scale of building a bridge, or a new airport, but you will still be responsible for taking small and medium-sized projects from con-ception to completion and here's some advice that might help you in this regard.

1. Why Do Projects Fail?

It's important to quickly identify some common reasons why projects of various sizes fail:

Bad Idea

Sometimes, as was clearly the case with the supermarket competition, the proj-ect is based on a bad idea or flawed thinking. No amount of effective planning or execution is going to change that fact. After that one eventful day, the super-market game disappeared, as if it had never happened. I wonder what level of resources was wasted on the whole project.

Bad Execution

This can involve a host of problems, including:

Ineffective leadership – if the person leading the project isn't on top of things then that will obviously impact on the quality of execution.

Poor team selection – managing a project will usually involve a team-based approach of some kind, and getting the right mix of personalities, expertise and commitment is always a challenge. I don't know the make-up of the team man-aging the supermarket competition, but something was clearly amiss in terms of their knowledge and skills, be that in relation to the competition itself, the tech-nology behind it, understanding the needs of the people it was targeted at, or simply a lack of appreciation of the nuts and bolts of project management.

Ineffective Communication

In any team situation communication is the key, but its importance is significantly magnified in a project scenario because team members frequently come from different parts of the organisation or even outside it, and they meet infrequently, so getting and keeping everyone on the same wavelength is even more difficult.

Poor Concept Testing

At various stages, concepts and ideas should be tested and even the end-product requires rigorous challenging before launch. Things can unexpectedly go wrong, particularly where technology is concerned, but it never ceases to amaze me just how many 'ready' projects fail to deliver once launched: the supermarket machine might have been tested, but probably not against the volume of use that was to be expected. Think too of the Apple Maps fiasco here as an example of how even global companies can get things wrong once they push the 'live' button; as you may remember, once up and running Apple Maps was found to be plagued by major geographical errors and bugs.

'Growing Legs'

Sometimes the project begins with a clear and simple concept but before you know it the thing starts to grow legs, i.e. people can stray from the agreed vision, or can get over-excited during the planning phase, which leads to far too many layers being added to the core concept. Maybe the supermarket competition started life as a simpler idea and someone got ahead of themselves.

There are many reasons why projects can go astray, so what can be done to minimise the risk of failure?

2. Planning to Succeed

As a manager, it is your job to develop an effective vision and plan for any projects you head up, and to do so in a way that seeks to address common pitfalls such as those mentioned above. Failing to effectively manage your projects can prove disastrous for your career at any time but especially so in an environment where any waste of resources is most certainly going to be noticed and the consequences magnified. Of course, there are many well-known project management systems, and a range of software supports available, some of which can be quite complex but one straightforward and widely used framework for project planning is the OARS approach ('objectives, activities, relationship and schedule')[81] which involves the following stages:

Define the *objectives* for the project to be undertaken. And of course, make sure your objectives are SMART:

- Specific
- Measurable
- Achievable
- Relevant
- Time bound

[81] Davies, *The Essentials of Management: 20 Tried and Tested Activities for Developing Best Practice* (Ely: Fenman 1999).

Figure 29.1   **A Sample Gantt Chart**

Pre-opening Tasks	May	June	July	Aug	Sept	Oct	Nov	Dec
Engage in detailed discussions with key stakeholders of the centre and agree memoranda of understanding with each	■							
Develop a financial model for the centre with detailed sources of funds, expenditure levels, grant and financial support measures and income streams		■						
Confer the legal status and authority of the centre to underpin its corporate remit and define the role and functions of the management board		■						
Select and appoint the chairperson and members of the management board in accordance with the articles of association			■					
Conduct awareness campaigns for attracting potential managers, employees and trainees				■				
Recruit and appoint the executive team, training staff, administrative and support personnel					■			
Prepare a detailed business plan for the centre and devise operating guidelines for each department						■		
Organise a workshop to implement pre-opening measures							■	
Recruit students								■

Always focus on your *objective*(s). Everything should be geared towards achieving them, there should be no ambiguity about what you are trying to deliver. For example, if you think again about the supermarket game – was the objective to reward customers, or to reward them in the most complex manner possible? Once defined, stick to what has been agreed.

List the major *activities* that have to be performed to achieve the objective(s). Brainstorming can be a useful tool here to help you flesh out all the key activities required to get from conception to completion. Then you need to analyse each major activity: can that activity be broken down into any smaller tasks that have to be completed before the major activity is finished?

Identify the *relationship* between activities and tasks. Does one activity have to be completed before another can be started? Put the activities and sub-tasks into a logical sequence. Then, work out a time-frame for each major activity and its sub-tasks. How long will each take from start to finish?

Develop a *schedule*. Work out the earliest start and latest finish dates for each activity. Identify which activities can be running at the same time and which can only be completed after something else finishes. Also identify who is responsible for each activity; make sure that the individuals concerned know where they fit into the game plan and precisely what area they are to be in charge of.

Use a planning tool such as a Gantt chart – a basic version of which is shown in **Figure 29.1** for the pre-opening of a training centre – to visualise the progression of the project.

This tried and tested approach to managing projects works well and I am sure that if you use the 'OARS' approach for planning the normal range of small and medium-scale projects that you will generally be responsible for, you will be less likely to fail, or indeed to find yourself standing red-faced as a project implodes in front of your eyes.

There is Only One Boss

"Hi, I'm really sorry about this, but my steak is far too tough to eat. And, it's also kind of cold."

"Oh, *ehm*, really? That's strange, because nobody else has complained about that tonight. (A response accompanied by rolling of eyes.)

"Well, thanks for sharing that with me and, honestly, I'm very happy for everyone else but I think it's too tough. And, as I said, it's lukewarm."

"So, what would you like me to do then, Sir?"

Biting tongue at this stage.

"How about you just get the manager for me, please …".

I made a complaint recently. It's something that I rarely do because it invariably causes more irritation than it's worth in terms of actually getting a resolution. But in this case the food was truly awful, we had waited forever, it was over-priced and the employees were unhelpful throughout, so I couldn't stop myself. I made the complaint, at least initially, in a genuinely polite manner and got the above reaction. Finally, the manager sauntered over and continued the intellectual debate about the precise definitions of 'tough' and 'tepid'. And the solution in the end? After several minutes of debate, with group participation, they wrote off my main course. How very innovative. Then the manager spent the rest of the time throwing dirty looks in my direction until we left.

Are the employees at this restaurant likely to have learned anything from the episode? Hardly. Did I? Yes, I most definitely did and one of them is that I won't be frequenting that particular place again. The incident did however get me focused on the issue of managing quality and, regardless of what field you are in, as a manager, it's always difficult to align what I call the four panes of the 'Quality Window', see **Figure 30.1**.

In essence, 'quality' in this context means ensuring that all aspects of your offering – your products and service – are designed, sold and delivered in a manner that exceeds expectations and provides real value for your customers; and that you have concrete evidence to verify that you have achieved that goal. Before honing in on the 'deliver' and 'listen' panes which will be the primary focus, here are some general points to consider about managing quality:

Figure 30.1   **The Quality Window**

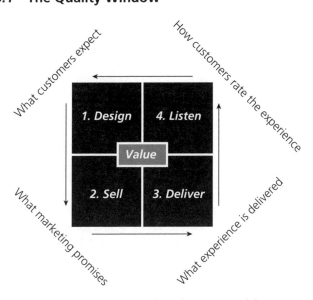
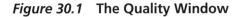

Try to Align the Four Panes as Closely as Possible

It's not easy to get that balance right, but failing to do so only leads to customer (individuals or other businesses) dissatisfaction and at best a short-term gain for your company. Think about how well you align the four panes in your organisation at present. As part of that reflection, it's important not to forget that promises are easily made and are communicated to customers in a variety of ways, through your brand values, marketing and promotion efforts, online and direct booking systems and even on a one-to-one basis. Consider how reflective your actual offering is when compared to the promises you make. It is not unusual in some companies to find that marketing personnel ('sell') and management/employees ('deliver') can be working with different goals in mind, so it is also worthwhile to think about whether there is any mismatch on that front in your business right now.

Try to Increase Choice, not Reduce it

In seeking to better align the four panes, it is important to also try to increase customer choice and not reduce it. Some companies today attempt to limit choice if they can get away with it, and this is an area where conflict between marketing and operations can arise. Marketers love choice, whereas operators like to (or are often forced to), limit it, because too much variety is seen as too difficult or costly to manage. It's difficult but not impossible, though. Customers like choice, and research shows they are prepared to pay a premium for it when those choices are attractive and delivered to a high standard.

Try to Really Understand Your Customers

Every business today says it understands its customers, but some are only kidding themselves. Maybe you do, and well done if so, but you should really think hard about how you feel you know those expectations. For example, how often do you conduct focus groups? How good are you at analysing and responding to customer feedback? How effective are those feedback systems – do they produce the quantity and quality of information you need? Are they designed to really help you develop comprehensive insights into your customers' expectations and evaluations, by segment? Or are they designed to make you feel good about yourselves by giving you a high score? How well are your products and services currently tailored to your customer segments? How do you stay in tune with their changing needs?

Be Strategic about Quality

Managers in every company, or certainly the better ones, talk about quality all the time but much of that talk is of a tactical nature and is focused on enhancing products and services on an on-going basis. This is good, necessary and indeed advisable. However, thinking strategically about managing quality – in a way that is reflective of a market leader in your sector – is a totally different matter and requires that the issue be fully integrated into your strategic decision-making process, brand management efforts, talent management strategy and indeed innovation initiatives.

Be Passionate about Quality

Think about how you and other managers, at all levels, view the issue of managing quality. Is it seen as something to be 'done' or 'managed', or is it a challenge that really drives you, individually and collectively? Do you have a genuine passion for it?

Engage Employees in the Effort

You will have heard plenty of talk about the subject of employee engagement, but a simple fact remains true: engaged employees deliver better service quality, which in turn generates loyal customers and ultimately improves financial performance. As former Campbell's Soup CEO, Doug Conant, once said, "To win in the marketplace you must first win in the workplace."[82]

The Quality Window is a simple but useful conceptual tool for all managers to discuss and consider the often opposing forces associated with managing quality. And of course value lies at the heart of that window, and although what your customers consider that to be will vary, you must always think about how you can add value for them rather than solely concentrating on price. In terms of managing quality across all aspects of what you offer, your attention naturally needs to be on all four panes, but as mentioned, the focus here will be specifically on the 'deliver' and 'listen' panes.

1. What Experience is Delivered?

Regardless of the field or sector that you are in, to manage quality effectively you will have to focus on your 'hotspots', those really essential components that

---

[82] Kruse, "What is Employee Engagement?" *Forbes,* 22 June 2012.

combine to form the overall customer experience. In any business, these hotspots
will include:

- *Product hotspots:* Which of course relate to whatever products you offer to
  your customers.
- *People hotspots:* Such as the service offered by your employees to your customers across all areas of the experience, from handling telephone enquiries or
  reservations, dealing with customers face-to-face, and responding to them when
  they make a complaint, or when they simply need guidance and support.
- *Physical hotspots:* For instance your facilities, if your customers come onsite
  to buy your products, or experience your service.
- *Promotional hotspots:* Such as how you 'interact' with customers through your
  visual displays, online or social media platforms, and other promotional material.

A product hotspot can be large or small, or involve a purchase requiring minor or
major decision-making. A personal hotspot may be brief, say when a customer asks
an employee for directions in-store, or more lengthy if they were asking a salesper-
son to explain the specification of a car they were considering buying. Physical
hotspots include how your premises look to customers; for instance, a dirty car
park can send the wrong message. A promotional hotspot can be the quality of
your website, or the attractiveness of a newspaper ad you place. Essentially, any
customer experience, in any business, is made up of a mixture of hotspots, each one
of which contributes in some way to the overall quality of the experience.

And again, regardless of your particular business, I am sure that you will agree
there is no issue more challenging for you as a manager than seeking to achieve
quality across all your hotspots. Yet getting your product, physical and promotional hotspots right is somewhat easier as they are 'controllable', in the sense
that you can plan, design and monitor them in a structured way. Managing the
personal hotspots – the service component – is far more challenging, however;
you might even say that service quality is the Holy Grail of all businesses. Every
owner and manager struggles with the service quality issue to some degree, and
no doubt you do too, perhaps spending significant time trying to ensure that
your employees handle each of the service interactions in a similar fashion,
doing the right things in the same helpful, friendly manner.

Change How You Look at this Area

Managing quality of service is difficult because people are not machines and
cannot be programmed to get it right every time. Recent decades have seen
many businesses identify their service hotspots and then seek to define responses
(standards and procedures), to them to the extent that in a lot of companies
today you find service manuals lined up on shelves bulging at the seams with
advice on the 'correct' way to do things, none of which are actually used on a
day-to-day basis. It's got to the point now that when you talk to employees and
indeed managers about service standards and procedures you can see their eyes
start to glaze over. And who can blame them? Words such as 'standard' or
'procedure' scream greyness and rigidity and they certainly don't instil any sense
of excitement or passion for service quality, do they? In fact, they are likely to
have the opposite effect.

Now, don't get me wrong, solutions to delivering consistent and high quality service have to be about more than massaging the terminology involved, but changing how you communicate the issue is not a cosmetic exercise. Think of it in simple terms – would you rather talk about service *standards* or a service *goal*? I know which one would matter more to me. So, in dealing with the issue of service quality, instead of talking to your people about standards (what you want to achieve) and procedures (what you have to do to achieve the standard required), consider speaking in terms of 'service goals'. In fact, I have seen first-hand how altering the packaging around this issue has made a big difference. Of course, there has to be substance under the fancy wrapping too, and here's how that can be achieved.

Defining Service Goals

The start point if you want to get better at managing the quality of your service hotspots is to define customer expectations for each and every one of them, and then translate those expectations into short, snappy goals. Let's take an example of a service hotspot that would be common to most businesses – handling a telephone enquiry:

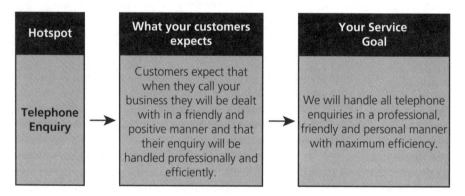

There's nothing earth shattering in the above, but for this particular hotspot the service goal is now very clear and more easily communicated to employees. The key point here is that the service goals you agree, as a first step, set the boundaries for what everyone involved is trying to achieve in terms of service quality. They are:

- Challenging because the aim is to achieve them all the time
- Relevant because they are based specifically on what customers generally expect
- Easy to communicate to employees because they simplify what it is they are trying to achieve for their customers.

The next issue is to then consider how much practical guidance to give your employees in what must be done to achieve each of the service goals you define. This, unfortunately, is where many businesses end up swamped in paperwork, because they define written procedures in great detail covering every possible eventuality. I don't think this approach works very well and, especially if you have an engaged group of people (and that's the crucial factor here), then all they need is guidance, not hand-holding. That direction can be provided by outlining the 'service steps' required to achieve each service goal through on-the-job training and coaching, rather than having written procedures for everything. If you still feel compelled to develop written service steps for the 'right way' to do things then keep them as brief as possible, but if your training is effective – and ongoing supervision is strong – then only having service goals should suffice.

The service goals approach offers just the right amount of guidance to engaged employees regarding what needs to be done to manage your service hotspots. If each one of your employees were constantly striving to achieve the service goals you set for all hotspots, then they would not only meet but likely exceed most customer expectations of service quality, particularly if employees are passionate and enthusiastic in their interactions. This again is why engagement is so vital.

To make a final point here, dealing with complaints should be seen as a critical service hotspot and you should have a clear service goal for this area. Your people should be fully trained in how to deal with complaints and they should be empowered to make decisions on the spot. All very simple stuff I know, but have you tried complaining lately?

2. How Do Customers Rate the Experience Offered?

Not so long ago, I was working with a group of managers to explore business improvement alternatives and, about half-way through the session, I annoyed some of them. But in doing so, hopefully I did them a favour as well.

"I'd say we're already a leader in that area," one of the group had said, as we got on to the issue of managing quality.

I love modesty and so I followed up with, "How do you know that?"

"Because our customers tell us that we are," responded two of the managers, almost in unison, and I saw the glance between them which indicated that they felt they were dealing with a complete moron.

"And how do they do that?" I asked.

"Because we use comment cards, and last year we had an 80% satisfaction rating; this year, so far, we have raised it to 85%."

"And how does that figure compare to the industry average?" I asked.

That last question was met only by silence. They didn't have an answer to it, nor in my experience, do many companies. From what I regularly see, when it comes to really measuring quality – be that product or service related – generating an internal feel-good factor in terms of the feedback attained is often more important than generating a truly accurate picture. This particular business is undoubtedly quite good at what they do, but they aren't anywhere near quality leaders no matter what they might like to think, and particularly so because:
- Relying on comment cards as the sole feedback mechanism is pointless because at best, comment cards are only completed by a small proportion of

the customer base; and often only from an extreme point of view: when they are either very happy or very disappointed with the experience.
- Equally, whilst measuring internal year-on-year feedback scores is of course vital, the result achieved is relatively meaningless unless it is externally benchmarked, and this applies not just to customer feedback scores but to anything measured. Increasing any result by 5% annually is better than a decrease naturally but, if the average industry performance for that particular metric is a 10% increase, then you have in reality under-performed.

The workshop incident got me thinking about measuring quality in general and particularly how to excel in this area. Too many companies believe they are better than they actually are in terms of quality and, as a result of having overly narrow measurement systems, they lull themselves into a false sense of security. And don't just take my word for it. A study on the issue by leading consultant Bain & Company[83] confirms the scale of misconceptions. The researchers commented: "When we recently surveyed 362 companies, we found that 80% believed they were delivering a 'superior experience' to their customers. But when we asked customers, they gave only 8% of the companies high marks." They also add generally about satisfaction ratings, "Our research shows there's actually little correlation between 'satisfaction' and consumer loyalty. We typically find that 80% of consumers who defect to competitors score themselves as 'satisfied' or 'very satisfied' on surveys – just before they jump ship. And that's not the only way in which the lens of satisfaction warps management perceptions. As an average measure, it doesn't delve into the differences among consumer segments."

Clearly, there are many enterprises around that do a great job of keeping their customers happy, and of measuring the scale of that happiness, but being a company that consistently provides above average quality, or is a real leader in this area, is another matter entirely. To truly measure the quality of the experience that you offer, you need a comprehensive approach that includes:
- Regular internal and external quality audits that objectively measure the quality of the actual experience offered from a customer's perspective across your product, physical, personal and promotional hotspots.
- A range of customer feedback channels that enable you to get both quantitative and qualitative data about how your customers rate what you offer, again across a range of hotspots and for all your key segments. These tools might include a combination of comment cards, face-to-face and online surveys, focus groups, targeted interviews and so on.

As part of your thinking about different approaches you can apply to measuring customer feedback, do you know what your 'Net Promoter Score' (NPS)[84] is? For

[83] Blasberg, Vishwanath and Allen, "Turning Your Consumers into Die-Hard Fans", at http://www.bain.com/publications/articles/turning-your-consumers-into-die-hard-fans. aspx
[84] Reichheld and Markey, *The Ultimate Question 2.0: How Net Promoter Companies Thrive in a Customer-Driven World* (Revised ed., Harvard Business Review Press 2011).

those unfamiliar with the concept, the Net Promoter Score is the result achieved when you survey your customers with the "would you recommend?" question. The concept was first developed by Frederick F. Reichheld[85] and a team from Bain & Co which examined the issue of customer satisfaction measurement. He found that many customer satisfaction surveys weren't of much use because they were often too long or cumbersome, with low response rates.

Whilst exploring the issue, Reichheld identified that Enterprise Rent-A-Car was using two simple questions to measure feedback: one about the quality of their rental experience and the other about the likelihood that the customer would rent from the company again. He wondered whether it was possible to get similar results in other industries – including those more complex sectors than car rentals – by focusing only on customers who provided the most enthusiastic responses to a short list of questions designed to assess their loyalty to a company. He further wondered whether the list could be reduced to a *single* question. If it could, what would that question be?[86]

It turned out that yes indeed, a single survey question could serve as a useful indicator of business growth. But that question wasn't about customer satisfaction or even loyalty, at least not in so many words. Instead, it was focused on a customer's willingness to recommend a product or service to someone else. Reichheld found that, in most of the industries he studied, the percentage of customers who were enthusiastic enough to refer a friend or colleague – perhaps the strongest sign of customer loyalty – correlated directly with differences in growth rates among competitors.

So that very briefly is where the NPS concept originated, and it's easy to calculate. When you ask the question of your customers, "On a scale of 0–10, how likely is it that you would recommend our company to a friend or colleague?" you identify three types of customer: 'detractors' (0–6), 'passives' (7–8) and 'promoters' (9–10). Then, when you subtract the percentage of 0s to 6s from the percentage of 9s and 10s, that gives you your NPS score as the diagram below shows:

How likely are you to recommend to a colleague or friend?

	Detractors						Passives		Promoters	
0	1	2	3	4	5	6	7	8	9	10

Not likely at all   *Neutral*   Extremely Likely

Adapted from www.netpromotor.com

Your Net Promoter Score is simply attained by subtracting the percentage of detractors (0–6s) from the percentage of promoters (9–10s).

---

[85] *Ibid.*
[86] Reichheld, "The One Number You Need to Grow" (2003) December, *Harvard Business Review*, pp. 46–54.

Using customer satisfaction as a measure is obviously fine but what Reichheld's research showed was that 'satisfaction' is not necessarily an indicator of 'loyalty', and it's the latter that actually drives business growth. The main reasons why NPS has grown in popularity as an indicator is that:

- It's easy to understand and calculate;
- It has been shown that loyalty is an indicator of likely future behaviour; and
- Customer loyalty levels are proven to be correlated to business growth levels.

According to Bain & Co, "to test the link between Net Promoter Scores and growth, research teams compiled scores for leading companies in a wide range of industries. What they found was compelling. Though the scores themselves varied widely by industry, Net Promoter leaders on average grew at more than twice the rate of competitors." Now, for all the positives, it has to be said that there are some who criticise the NPS, believing it to be overly simplistic and arguing that one question can never summarise the totality of the customer experience. Still, it remains a widely-used tool across the business world and, if you haven't considered it already, it's worth further exploration, but only, of course, in the context of the comprehensive approach to measuring quality mentioned earlier.

The focus here has been on managing quality which is a real challenge for any manager and the key message is that whatever you do, keep things relatively simple in how you view, and then manage, this important area. The Quality Window is a useful conceptual framework to guide your discussions on how best to align four key activities which combine to help you gain competitive advantage in terms of the quality you offer. And, after all, nothing matters more than exceeding your customers' expectations, especially today.

As Sam Walton, Founder of Wal-Mart, once said "There is only one boss. The customer. And he can fire everybody in the company from the chairman on down, simply by spending his money somewhere else."

Conclusion

I hope that this book has afforded you an opportunity to take a step back from your busy life as a manager and, in light of all the new realities you face, to reflect upon important aspects of what you do; and in the process to provide you with some current research and practical insights to guide those reflections. It begins with a focus on your own strengths and areas for improvement and stresses the need, regardless of your level of experience, to keep reaching higher in terms of expanding your competences and capabilities: in other words, if you want to get the best out of others, you must continuously stretch yourself first.

The second area of attention is that of your employees. No matter what field you are in, it is people who make the difference between an average business and one that excels. Sure, the quality and appeal of your products and services are vital success factors too, as are many other issues, but it is in how your employees develop and deliver your offering, or in how they approach their work, that you can really put some clear water between your business and the competition; principles, products, and processes can be easily copied, not so people. And it is not an exaggeration to say that employees demand a lot more from their working life than previously, but that is a good thing because it forces you to constantly enhance the employment experience.

Finally, the third area of focus is on important aspects of running your business, or area, ranging from strategic planning to managing quality. The common thread across all of those topics is that, where possible, you should try to reduce complexity in how they are viewed and applied in your business. After all, simple doesn't have to mean simplistic, and by and large people prefer – and respond better to – plain speaking and easy-to-understand concepts.

In addressing all these topical issues, there has been no attempt to tell you how you should manage for best effect, but rather to expose you to a range of insights and perspectives that can help you to reflect upon your current approach and then make some decisions in response. What you now do with the knowledge gained is of course entirely up to you, but doing nothing should never be an option. I think the words of Richard Branson sum up very well the attitude we all need to take towards the personal and management development journey: "My biggest motivation? Just to keep challenging myself. I see life almost like one long university education that I never had – every day I'm learning something new." This captures nicely what is needed and hopefully my book has helped you to learn something new about yourself, your employees and your business, which you can now translate into practical action.

Thank you and I wish you every future success.

EL